There is a Season

Experiencing Contentment
in Every Season of Life

Laurie Cole

Production Coordinators: Janet Valentine, Pam Henderson
Layout and Design: Pam Henderson
Editors: Lee Valentine, Robin Cook
Art Director: Scott Head
Photography: Don and Mary Carico, Lakewood Photography

Third Edition—2007

Priority Ministries
Encouraging Women to Give God Glory & Priority

www.priorityministries.org

This book is lovingly dedicated to my parents, *John and Julia McKay*, who instilled in me, at a very early age, a love and reverence for God and His Word, and modeled for me what it means to love God and to live His Word in every season of life.

Acknowledgements

At the invitation of a dear friend, **Janet Valentine**, God provided me the opportunity to prepare this study for the Lifetouch Ladies' Bible Study at my home church, Sagemont Church, in Houston, Texas. Having never written a Bible study like this, I had no idea of the mountainous multitude of details that would be involved. But with Janet's encouraging words, "Laurie, you just write the study, and I'll take care of the details," I began writing. And Janet…well she, indeed, took care of the details or this workbook would most assuredly not be in your hands! Thank you, Janet, for getting this project going and for lovingly and tirelessly seeing it through to its completion.

When I began this workbook, I also had no idea of the need there would be for so many others to assist me—but God did, and He moved the hearts of others to help. It was an honor and a joy to co-labor with them, and I owe each of the following key people an enormous debt of gratitude:

Pam Henderson, a godly, treasured friend who is also a highly organized, highly skilled word-processor/layout and design extraordinaire. Pam took my messy manuscripts and (almost miraculously) turned them into a beautiful workbook.

Scott Head, a gifted and creative graphic designer who generously, patiently, and selflessly contributed his time and considerable talent to this project and whose encouragement was so timely throughout the entire production process.

Lee Valentine (Janet's husband), a skilled grammarian, proofreader, and copy editor who prayerfully read each word of the rough manuscripts and then "smoothed-out" each page with his "eagle-eye" corrections and insightful suggestions.

Robin Cook, who was one of the very first participants of this study when it was piloted at my home church, gave me honest feedback from a student's perspective, excellent editorial insights and, best of all, became a new and cherished friend of mine in the process.

Karen Jackson and **Lezli Busbee**, two beloved friends of mine, who carved out substantial amounts of time from their busy schedules to proofread this workbook because of their love for the Lord and His Word.

Finally, I would like to thank my sweet husband, **Bill**, and my wonderful sons, **David**, **Kevin**, and **J.J.**, for their encouragement and for the sacrifices they willingly made which ultimately made it possible for me to complete this project. Never once did they complain about my shoddy housework and the deficit of home-cooked meals they missed during the months I was writing. Guys, I was able to write this book guilt-free because of your unconditional love. Now I know you probably didn't even notice the messy house, but I promise to dust off the stove-top and fire-up the oven very soon.

About the Study

This workbook is an in-depth, topical Bible study. It is designed to enable you to "dig-in" to God's Word and experience the joy of discovering truth as the Holy Spirit tutors and teaches you through the scriptures. To facilitate your sensitivity and dependence upon the Spirit, each day you will be encouraged (through a verse from Psalm 119) to begin your study in prayer and, at the conclusion of each day's study, you will be instructed to record any insights the Holy Spirit has given you.

A good translation of the Bible will be essential as you do this study. The *New American Standard*, the *New International Version*, the *King James Version*, or *New King James Version* are all very accurate translations and are highly recommended.

Please note that this workbook contains fill-in-the-blank listening guides with each lesson. These listening guides are designed to be compatible with the *There is a Season* audio CD and video DVD lectures taught by Laurie Cole and may be purchased online at www.priorityministries.org.

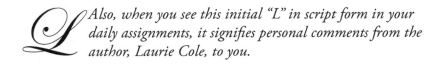 *Also, when you see this initial "L" in script form in your daily assignments, it signifies personal comments from the author, Laurie Cole, to you.*

About the Author

Laurie Cole is the Founder and President of Priority Ministries, a ministry dedicated to encouraging and equipping women to love God most and seek Him first. Raised in a strong Christian home, Laurie became a Christian at an early age. But in her early twenties, God tested and taught her the importance of truly giving Him priority in her life.

In 1985, Laurie enrolled in an in-depth women's Bible study. Encouraged by the older women who led the study, Laurie received training and began teaching and leading a group where God affirmed His call upon her life to teach. For over 20 years, Laurie has taught dozens of Bible studies, spoken at numerous women's events and conferences, and is the author of two other in-depth Bible studies: *Beauty by THE BOOK* and *The Temple*. Her passion for God and hunger for His Word continues to grow.

A minister's wife, Laurie and her husband, Bill, serve the Lord at Sagemont Church in Houston, Texas, where he is the Associate Pastor of Worship and Praise. They have been married for over 30 years and have three sons (David, Kevin, and J.J.), one beloved daughter-in-law (Stephanie), and two glorious grandchildren (Ezra and Juliette).

Contents

Introduction

Many years ago, God placed this book on my heart, but it was not the proper season for me to write. Year after year, season after season, God's call was ever present, but His timing was unclear.

Fifteen years ago when I first began studying the seasons of life, the truths I learned gave me a new perspective on life. Since that time and with every passing season, God has continued to teach me the beauty and the significance of Ecclesiastes 3:1:

> *To every thing there is a season, and a*
> *time to every purpose under the heaven.*

God's call, all those years ago, to write this study was very real. Back then, I thought I was ready to fulfill that call. But God knew better. He knew I was not ready. In fact, God had some long-range demolition and reconstruction work scheduled for my life before He would ever enable me to fulfill His call to write this study.

A few months ago, at the invitation of a friend to write a Bible study for her women's group, a kind of domino effect began to occur. God was making His timing *crystal clear*. It was time to write.

My sister, I don't know what season of life you're currently experiencing, but I invite you to come with me on a journey into the Word of God that could potentially transform your heart and every remaining season of your life. And trust me, if He can transform me, He can transform you, too.

Your sister,

Laurie

Thou hast turned for me my mourning into dancing;
Thou has loosed my sackcloth and girded me with gladness;
That my soul may sing praise to Thee, and not be silent, O Lord
my God, I will give thanks to Thee forever. Psalm 30:11-12

Getting Honest: Are You Content?

I. **Our destination:** _____

    A. **Our Itinerary:**

        1. The first part of our journey will involve _____ and
_____ the seasons of life in order to:

            • discover your own _____ season of life, and to

            • gain insight about God's _____ throughout the seasons
of your life.

        2. The second part of our journey will involve learning the _____
of _____ in order to:

            • _____ them to your life in every _____;

            • and to ultimately _____ _____
in every remaining season of your life.

    B. **Defining Our Destination:**
_____: to be _____ with your _____,
_____ or _____.

    C. **Our Starting Point:** We know the destination, but, in order to get there, we must first
_____ _____ where we are right now.

II. **Job's Journey:**

    A. *Job 1:1–3*—Job's Description:
spiritually = _____, _____, Godfearing
physically = _____ and _____.
Result: _____.

    B. *Job 1:20–22, 2:10*—Job's Initial Response to Satan's Attacks:
he _____ and worshipped, _____ God,
did not _____ , did not _____ God.

    C. *Job 3–31*—Job's Eventual Response:
spiritually = _____.
physically = in pain and _____.
Result: _____.

    D. Two Truths:

        1.   _____ _____ can cause even the _____,
most godly believer to experience discontent.

        2. _____ believers will ever experience the _____ suffering Job did, yet
many of us are discontent when we experience even _____ suffering.

III.   **The Question: Why do so few Christian women experience ongoing contentment?**

Cole's Unscientific Conclusions: 3 Groups of Women

    A.   **Group 1—Contentment** _____: This group of women continually repeat
a _____ _____ seeking satisfaction in many things.

        Result: _____.

    B.   **Group 2—Contentment** _____: This group of women have chased
contentment but have found it to be only _____.

        Result: _____.

    C.   **Group 3—**_____: This rare group of women have discovered real
_____, _____, and _____ despite their season
of life or their circumstances.

        Result: _____

IV.   **The Answer: If we want to experience ongoing contentment in every season of our life,
we must—**

    A.   _____ _____ with ourselves.

    B.   If necessary, _____ our sin and _____. *Job 42:1-6*

    C.   _____ and _____ the scriptural principles of contentment.
Phil. 4:11-12

There is a Season Part I

Identifying and Understanding
the Seasons of Life

She Said He Said:
Proverbs 31 vs. Ecclesiastes 1

Have you ever seen a reflection of yourself from…well, let's just say, a less-than-flattering angle? Like when you're out shopping and you see yourself in one of those three-way mirrors? You left home thinking, "I don't look too bad. I'm presentable enough to go out in public. In fact, I look just fine." But later as you're casually browsing in the women's department, you stroll by a three-way mirror. Outwardly your mouth drops open. Inwardly you gasp in horror! You're now seeing yourself from every possible angle—front, side, and rear! Immediately you ask yourself, "What was I thinking leaving the house looking like this!? Where was my mind when I bought this sleeveless blouse—my arms are gigantic!? And these pants—no wonder they were so difficult to zip! Why it's amazing they didn't split wide open when I got into the car!" Instantly the shopping trip is over, and the diet has begun!

Three-way mirrors—unless you're Julia Roberts—are probably *not* your best friend. Mirrors often reveal far more than we're prepared to see. I can vividly remember a time in my life fifteen years ago when God held a mirror up before me. As I looked into that mirror, I was shocked to see the reflection of the person I had become. I saw bitterness, cynicism, a self-centered attitude, and many, many extra pounds of discontent. Of course, God's mirror wasn't a literal mirror. The mirror He used was the mirror of His Word. The Bible says:

> *For if anyone is a hearer of the word and not a doer,*
> *he is like a man who looks at his natural face in a mirror;*
> *for once he has looked at himself and gone away, he has*
> *immediately forgotten what kind of person he was. But the one*
> *who looks intently at the perfect law, the law of liberty, and abides*
> *by it, not having become a forgetful hearer, but an effectual doer,*
> *this man shall be blessed in what he does.* James 1:23–25

God's Word is like a high-quality mirror. When we look intently at it, we will see God's standard and whether or not we are a reflection of that standard. Just like that moment before the three-way mirror in the women's department, we may be stunned by the reality of what we see as we look intently into the mirror of God's Word.

A literal mirror may or may not reveal our true physical flaws. In fact, some mirrors are "magic" mirrors. These are the ones we all love because they've been hung at a very slight angle that makes a very big difference. When we look into these kinds of mirrors we think, "Wow, I'm taller *and* slimmer than I thought I was!" But God's mirror—the Bible—is perfect. It will never lie to us. When we look at it, we will always see the truth about ourselves—and we will be forced to make a decision. We'll either choose to walk away and ignore the spiritually out-of-shape person we've become, or we'll choose to embrace the truth and allow God to shape us into His image.

In this first week's lesson, you'll be standing before the same mirror God used in my life fifteen years ago: Proverbs 31 and Ecclesiastes 1–2. I want to encourage you to look *intently* into His mirror. Some of the scriptures you'll be studying may be very familiar to you, and you might be tempted to breeze through them more quickly than you should. Take your time. Read and re-read these passages. Commit to become "an effectual doer" of God's Word and not a "forgetful hearer." And let me remind you of the wonderful promise to the one
who is "an effectual doer" of the Word: "This man shall be blessed in what he does."

Study intently this week, my sister. Choose to be blessed!

Day One

1. Begin your study in prayer. Ask the Lord to guide and teach you by His Spirit. Commit to walk in the truth He reveals, and claim the blessing of Psalm 119:1.

   How blessed are those whose way is blameless
   who walk in the law of the LORD. Psalm 119:1

2. Proverbs 31:10–31 describes the woman many Christians and theologians call "the model woman." Using your Bible, read through this passage slowly and deliberately—in other words, intently.

3. In the space provided below, describe your first impressions of Proverbs 31:10–31. Be honest. Were you inspired as you read? Or were you just tired as you read? She is one hardworking woman, isn't she? As you looked into this "mirror," what did you see, and how did it make you feel?

4. Read through Proverbs 31:10–31 again, and make notes in the following categories listed below. Use your own words as well as words from the text, and be sure to note the verse to which your notes refer.

THE MODEL WOMAN

Describe her relationships.
Describe the various components of her life such as how she spends her time and the things she does.
Describe her attitude and outlook toward her life, her work, and her future.
Describe her relationship with God and how it impacts her life.

5. Read through Proverbs 31:10–31 one last time and note the following:

    a. In what ways are you like this woman? What attributes does she possess that you also possess? How is her life like yours? How are her relationships like yours?

    b. In what ways are you unlike her? What attributes does she possess that you do not possess? How is her life unlike yours? How are her relationships unlike yours?

c. How easy or how difficult is it for you to relate to her? Explain your answer.

d. Do you think this passage represents "A Day in the Life of the Proverbs 31 Woman," or do you think the passage paints a panoramic portrait of a woman throughout the many seasons of her life? Explain your answer.

Thy word is a lamp to my feet, and a light to my path.
Psalm 119:105

The unfolding of Thy words gives light.
Psalm 119:130

6. Finally, record what the Holy Spirit has revealed to you today as you've looked into the mirror of His Word. What insight has He given you for your own personal application?

_____

_____

_____

_____

_____

_____

_____

_____

_____

Day Two

1. Begin your study in prayer. Ask the Holy Spirit to guide you as you observe His Word. Commit to seeking Him with your whole heart.

How blessed are those who observe His testimonies, who seek Him with all their heart. Psalm 119:2

2. For the next several days, you will be studying Ecclesiastes. Before you get started, it will be helpful to collect some background material and to do a brief character study on Solomon, the author of Ecclesiastes. Please read through the following passages noting any insights you learn about Solomon.

a. 1 Kings 2:10–12—What did you learn about Solomon's heritage?

b.   1 Kings 3:1–15—What did you learn about Solomon's relationship with the Lord and his character?

c.   1 Kings 4:29–34—What did you discover about Solomon's wisdom?

d.   1 Kings 5:1–5, 6:14—What did Solomon desire and do for God?

e.   1 Kings 8:57–61—What did Solomon desire for himself and his people in their relationship with God?

3. Read 1 Kings 11:1–13, and note what you learn about Solomon's ultimate downfall.

4. Solomon wrote Ecclesiastes during the latter part of his life. Read Ecclesiastes 1 and answer the following questions.
    a.   How would you describe Solomon's attitude at this point in his life?

b. What conclusions does Solomon make about life in Ecclesiastes 1?

c. Do you agree with Solomon's conclusions about life? Explain your answer.

*Thy word is a lamp
to my feet, and a
light to my path.*
Psalm 119:105

*The unfolding of Thy
words gives light.*
Psalm 119:130

5. Finally, record any "light" the Holy Spirit has given you today as you have looked into the mirror of His Word. What insight has He given you for your own personal application as you have studied the life of Solomon?

_____

_____

_____

_____

_____

_____

_____

_____

Day Three

1. Before you begin your study, take time to pray. Incorporate the scriptures from Psalm 119:5–6 into your prayer. Let it be your heart's cry:

    *Oh, that my ways may be established to keep
    Thy statutes! Then I shall not be ashamed when
    I look upon all Thy commandments.* Psalm 119:5–6

2. As you scan Ecclesiastes 1, you'll see the word "vanity" is frequently used. It occurs over 30 times in the book of Ecclesiastes making it the key word of the entire book. The Bible is a divinely inspired book (2 Peter 1:20–21). Each word within its pages was individually and specifically chosen by God. In order for us to understand God's message in the book of Ecclesiastes, we need to understand the definition of the word "vanity."

Using any secular or Bible dictionaries you have, look up the word "vanity," and record its definition in the following space. You also may find it helpful to read several other Bible translations and note how the word "vanity" is translated in them. If you have an Amplified Bible, it is especially helpful.

3. Solomon uses a descriptive phrase to illustrate what vanity is like. Read the following scriptures and write out that repeated phrase on the line provided below.

    a. Ecclesiastes 1:14   d. Ecclesiastes 2:17

    b. Ecclesiastes 1:17   e. Ecclesiastes 2:26

    c. Ecclesiastes 2:11

    Repeated Phrase: _____

4. Take a moment to visualize mentally what it would look like for someone to physically act out this descriptive phrase. Explain how this phrase describes and illustrates vanity.

5. The book of Ecclesiastes reveals that Solomon, the wisest man who ever lived, an immensely powerful king, the successful leader of Israel, a man of vast wealth and immeasurable possessions, sought the exact same things endless others have pursued: *true meaning and lasting satisfaction in life*. Despite the fact he had everything anyone could ever possibly want, Solomon was dissatisfied and disillusioned with life.

    Read Ecclesiastes 1:2–3, and write your own personal paraphrase of these verses. Using your own words, how would you express Solomon's statement (verse 2) and question (verse 3)?

6. Proverbs 31 is the final chapter of that book. The very next book in the Bible is Ecclesiastes. In some Bibles, Proverbs 31 is on the left-hand page and Ecclesiastes 1 is on the right-hand page. Your Bible may not have the same layout, but please keep in mind that when Proverbs 31 ends, Ecclesiastes immediately follows.

   Scan Proverbs 31:10–31 and Ecclesiastes 1, and answer the following questions:

   a. Did you note any difference in the attitude and life experiences of the Proverbs 31 woman and Solomon? If so, please explain.

   b. Does Proverbs 31 seem to contradict the Ecclesiastes 1 passage? If so, how?

7. We'll close our study today with a couple of questions for personal reflection:

   a. Have you ever felt like Solomon? Have you ever thought, "Life is just a vicious cycle?" If so, write out what you were experiencing during that season of your life and the specific ways in which life seemed vain.

   b. Whose outlook and attitude do you relate to at this point in your life: the Proverbs 31 woman or Solomon? Explain your answer.

Thy word is a lamp to my feet, and a light to my path.
Psalm 119:105

The unfolding of Thy words gives light.
Psalm 119:130

Insights

8. Finally, record any "light" the Holy Spirit has given you today.

_____

_____

_____

_____

_____

_____

_____

_____

Day Four

1. Begin your day of study in prayer. Spend some time praising Him for the truths He has shown you and for the work He is doing in your life.

Blessed art Thou, O LORD; teach me Thy statutes…
I have rejoiced in the way of Thy testimonies…
I shall delight in Thy statutes… Psalm 119:12–16

Over the past two days, you've studied Solomon's cynical conclusion about life. He stated it in Ecclesiastes 1:2: "Vanity of vanities! All is vanity." The remainder of the book is dedicated to proving this conclusion. But the very first proof Solomon provides is his own personal experience.

Today we're going to study the various ways Solomon pursued meaning and satisfaction in life. You'll probably relate to some of these pursuits, and you'll certainly see that people haven't changed much since Solomon's day. Although our resources (both mental and material) may be limited compared to Solomon's, we've all pursued meaning and purpose in life in our own individual way.

2. Please read Ecclesiastes 1:16–2:17, and notice the long list of things Solomon diligently pursued in his quest for meaning in life.

3. Complete the following chart by reading the scripture reference. List Solomon's pursuit, and note the various ways you have sought this same pursuit. Also list the numerous ways people in our culture continue to pursue these same things. As an example, the first category has been started for you.

Searching for Satisfaction

Read	Solomon Pursued	How I've Pursued This	How Others Pursue This
a. Ecc. 1:16–18	wisdom	education	education
		reading	college/degrees
		Bible studies	therapists/Dr. Phil
b. Ecc. 2:1–2			

SEARCHING FOR SATISFACTION

READ	SOLOMON PURSUED	HOW I'VE PURSUED THIS	HOW OTHERS PURSUE THIS
c. Ecc. 2:3	_____	_____	_____
	_____	_____	_____
	_____	_____	_____
	_____	_____	_____
d. Ecc. 2:4–6	_____	_____	_____
	_____	_____	_____
	_____	_____	_____
	_____	_____	_____
e. Ecc. 2:7–8a	_____	_____	_____
	_____	_____	_____
	_____	_____	_____
	_____	_____	_____
f. Ecc. 2:8b	_____	_____	_____
	_____	_____	_____
	_____	_____	_____
	_____	_____	_____

4. Now take a moment to describe any pursuits that have been meaningful and satisfying in your life.

5. Describe how or why these things have brought meaning and satisfaction in your life.

6. Conclude this day of study by noting any insights the Holy Spirit has given you today.

_____

_____

_____

_____

_____

_____

_____

_____

Thy word is a lamp to my feet, and a light to my path.
Psalm 119:105

The unfolding of Thy words gives light.
Psalm 119:130

Day Five

1. Begin your time of study in prayer and by making Psalm 119:11 your goal.

Thy word I have treasured in my heart, that I may not sin against Thee. Psalm 119:11

2. Our final day of homework will be a study on the topic of contentment. First, please read the following definitions of contentment:

content¹	Satisfied; happy.
contentment²	The state of being contented.
contentment	To be satisfied; manifesting satisfaction with one's possessions, status, or situation.

3. Read the following verses and write out what you learn about contentment/satisfaction:

   a.   Psalm 107:1 and 9

    b.   Proverbs 19:23

    c.   Philippians 4:11–13

    d.   1 Timothy 6:6–8

    e.   Hebrews 13:5–6

4.   As you reflect upon the woman you studied in Proverbs 31 and the definition of contentment, would you define her as a woman of contentment? Briefly explain your answer.

5.   As you reflect upon Solomon from your studies in Ecclesiastes, would you define him as a man of contentment? Briefly explain your answer.

6. As you will recall, the key repeated word and theme of Ecclesiastes is "vanity," which is defined as "emptiness; fig. something transitory and unsatisfactory." [3] **Contentment, then, is the _opposite_ of vanity. Contentment results in satisfaction. Vanity results in dissatisfaction.**

   In what areas of your life are you most satisfied and content?

   In what areas of your life are you most dissatisfied and discontent? What areas of your life seem vain, empty, and without meaning?

We'll conclude each week's lesson in this study by journaling. I find journaling is a tool God uses to help me: (1) honestly express myself; (2) process and understand myself and the seasons and circumstances of my life; and (3) understand what God is seeking to teach and do in my life.

7. Take time to reflect upon what God has shown you this week and the way you sense He is working in your life. Journal your thoughts by completing the sentences provided.

My Journal

THIS WEEK THE LORD...

_____

_____

_____

_____

_____

_____

_____

_____

_____

_____

AS A RESULT, I...

_____
_____
_____
_____
_____
_____
_____
_____
_____
_____

Y ou've spent a lot of time this week gazing into the mirror of God's Word. Whatever the Lord has revealed to you, be assured of His unchanging love for you, and take heart in His abiding promise to you:

> *For I am confident of this very thing, that He*
> *who began a good work in you will perfect it*
> *until the day of Christ Jesus.* Philippians 1:6

Fifteen years ago when I saw my reflection in the mirror of the same verses you studied this week, I was shocked and ashamed. I was a professing Christian and a Bible teacher, yet I had become almost as cynical as Solomon. Reading Proverbs 31 did not inspire me, it only defeated and convicted me. But today I can testify to the faithfulness of God's promise from Philippians 1:6. Although I've still got a long way to go in my Christian walk, God forgave my sinful, negative attitude and began to teach me the principles of contentment—principles that have transformed my mind and become essential to me through the constantly changing seasons of my life.

This week you took God's mirror and saw the truth about yourself. Perhaps what you saw in the mirror wasn't very pretty. But here's some good news: God can perform spiritual "makeovers" in our lives! Over the next nine weeks, you will learn the principles of contentment. You will discover how to experience true joy, lasting satisfaction, and real meaning in every season of your life. And just think: at the conclusion of this study you may even be able to go to the mirror of Proverbs 31 and see a woman who looks at lot like...**YOU!**

She Said He Said: Proverbs 31 vs. Ecclesiastes 1

I. **The Model Woman—*Prov. 31:10–31***

    A. Is a _____ _____ of a woman through the _____ of her life.

    B. She lives a life of _____, _____, and _____.
    Prov. 31:13, 18, 25, 29

II. **Solomon—*Ecc. 1:1–14***

    A. Is the _____ _____ Solomon wrote during the _____ seasons of his life.

    B. He lives a life of _____, _____, and _____. *Ecc. 1:2–3, 8, 13b, 14*

III.

    <u>**Searching for Satisfaction:**</u>   <u>**A Scriptural Perspective:**</u>

    A. Wisdom—*Ecc. 1:16–17*   **A. Wisdom—*1 Cor. 1:18–24, 30***

- _____
- _____
- _____
- _____

    B. Pleasure—*Ecc. 2:1–2*   **B. Pleasure—*2 Tim. 3:1, 4, Titus 3:3, 1 Tim. 6:17***

- _____
- _____
- _____
- _____

    C. Alcohol/Drugs—*Ecc. 2:3*   **C. Alcohol/Drugs—*1 Tim. 5:23, Rom. 14:21, Eph. 5:18***

- _____
- _____
- _____
- _____

<u>**Searching for Satisfaction:**</u> <u>**A Scriptural Perspective:**</u>

D. Works/Projects—*Ecc. 2:4–6*

- _____
- _____
- _____
- _____

D. Works/Projects—*Col. 3:23, Luke 10:40–42*

- _____
  _____
- _____
  _____

E. Possessions/Money—*Ecc. 2:7–9*

- _____
- _____
- _____

E. Possessions/Money—*Mt. 6:19–21, 2 Tim. 6:6-8*

- _____
  _____
- _____
  _____

F. Sex—*Ecc. 2:8b*

- _____
- _____
- _____

F. Sex—*Heb. 13:4, 1 Cor. 6:18–20*

- _____
  _____
- _____
  _____
- _____
  _____

IV.   Final Conclusions:

A.   Life is _____ and a "chasing after the wind" when it is centered around
_____, _____ pursuits. *Ecc. 2:11*

B.   But, a life of _____, _____, and _____
can be experienced because Christ has redeemed us from _____.
1 Pet. 1:17b–19, 1 Cor. 15:58

The Seasons of Life

Ordinarily, I just love church. Fellowshipping with others, singing and worshipping the Lord, hearing a good sermon, returning home feeling uplifted and encouraged—what's not to love about that? Church is usually like having my spiritual batteries recharged. But let me be honest with you. There are times when church can be…well…*the most miserable place on earth*. It's true. After all, church can sometimes be a very convicting place. And on those Sundays, church is neither encouraging nor uplifting. In fact, when God is confronting me with my sin, I find church can be the most downright miserable place I could ever be!

I vividly recall one miserable day I spent in a church service fifteen years ago. I had "faked it" all through Sunday school the hour before, pretending everything was just fine in my own little world, but I simply did not have the strength to perform for one more hour. I purposefully chose to sit by myself in the most remote location I could find in our church auditorium. I mouthed the words to all the songs. I listened distractedly to the choir and soloist. The pastor preached, but I didn't hear a word. With my Bible opened in my lap, my mind was completely fixated on two passages that seemed to stare me down: Proverbs 31 and Ecclesiastes 1.

On one page, I saw a woman who had it all. She had a husband who adored and respected her, a life at home she found fulfilling, a successful career, and children who expressed gratitude and appreciation to her. She was the epitome of optimism, a woman who believed her life was meaningful. She was the perfect personification of contentment and satisfaction.

But on the opposite page, I saw a man who also had it all. He had more wisdom, riches, and power than anyone else in his entire kingdom. He should have been the happiest man alive. Yet he bluntly and honestly described his life as futile, empty, and meaningless. He was the epitome of cynicism. He was the perfect personification of dissatisfaction and disillusionment.

As I looked at the woman in Proverbs 31, I remembered how I used to feel inspired when I read about her. But now as I read Proverbs 31 I callously thought, "Yeah, right. This woman is fiction!" Instead, I much preferred the person described on the opposite page of my Bible who said, "Vanity of vanities! All is vanity. What advantage does man have in all his work which he does under the sun?" "Amen!" I thought, "That brilliant man in Ecclesiastes (unlike the Proverbs 31 woman) understands what life is really like for a thirty-something woman like me." His words—written right on the pages of my Bible—resonated with me and affirmed my own pessimistic philosophy about life.

But the affirmation I felt was extremely short-lived. As I sat there in church that day, a flood of conviction began to overwhelm my heart. God would not allow me to entertain or justify my cynical attitude for one more minute. He confronted me with my sin, and I was *miserable*.

Conviction, however, wasn't the only thing I felt. I was also puzzled and confused. A nagging, persistent question hounded my mind. How could one page of scripture teach that life is fulfilling, joyous, and satisfying and the very next page of scripture teach that life is futile, empty, and meaningless? Yet there they were standing side-by-side in scripture: Proverbs 31 and Ecclesiastes 1. To me, it seemed like those two pages completely contradicted one another.

In the midst of my confusion, God reminded me of a basic principle of Bible study: scripture cannot contradict scripture. Second Peter 1:21 says, "for no prophecy was ever made by an act of human will, but men moved by the Holy Spirit spoke from God." God is the true author of His Word. Through the power of His Spirit, He inspired each and every word. Therefore, because He is a perfect and holy God, He cannot contradict Himself. He cannot say one thing on one page of His Word and then say an entirely different thing on the next page.

Though convicted and confused, I knew there was only one thing to do: study, and study hard! I had to understand these passages. I *had* to figure out what was going on in my own personal life. I left church that day with a mission: to seek understanding for my confusion and healing for my convicted, hardened heart.

God was amazingly faithful and incredibly patient with me as I began my study of Proverbs 31 and Ecclesiastes 1. He took my cynical, disillusioned heart and made it tender and trusting again. And by His Spirit through His Word, He showed me something: Proverbs 31 and Ecclesiastes 1 absolutely do *not* contradict one another. In fact, they actually complement one another.

As I studied during that season of discontentment, God also gave me insight and understanding into the problems I was experiencing in my own personal life. At age thirty-five, I was plagued by some deeply disturbing questions such as:

- What had happened to me?
- How had I become so hardened and embittered?
- Why was I so disillusioned and discontent with my life?
- Would I ever experience true joy and find life meaningful and fulfilling again?

Perhaps you've asked some of those same questions yourself. Or maybe you've never experienced a season in your life where you've even thought about those kinds of questions. Whether or not you've ever experienced a "season of despair," this one thing I know: seasons change—whether we want them to or not! Therefore, we all need to be prepared for "winter" when our hearts will be imperiled by the icy, cold realities of life's trials and sorrows.

This week we will begin studying the seasons of life. I want you to understand what God's Word has to say about the various seasons and what they all share in common. I also want you to understand the impact these seasons will have upon your physical, emotional, and spiritual life. My prayer for you, dear sister, is that God will give you two things: (1) insight to enable you to discern the current season of your life and (2) faith to trust Him through every remaining season of your life. Study well…winter often comes without warning.

Day One

1. Begin your time of study in prayer and praise using Psalm 119:12 as your guide.

   Blessed art Thou, O Lord;
   Teach me Thy statutes. Psalm 119:12

2. This week our study will be centered on Ecclesiastes 3:1–8. Thoughtfully read through this passage.

3. Ecclesiastes 3:1 may be a very familiar verse to you, but please meditate upon it for a few moments to observe and absorb the truth it contains. Record your insights about this verse or restate it in your own words.

4. According to Ecclesiastes 3:1, is there anything or any event that does not have an appointed time or season? Please circle your answer: Yes   No

5. Read Genesis 8:20–22 and record your answers to the following questions:

   a.   Who is speaking in these verses?

   b.   What types of seasons are mentioned in verse 22? In other words, are these literal or figurative seasons?

6. Read Leviticus 26:3–4 and answer the following questions:

   a.   Who is speaking in these verses?

   b.   What promise is found in verse 4?

   c.   Is there a condition to this promise? If so, please record it below.

  d. How did God use the weather to speak to the Israelites?

 7. Read Psalm 27:4–5 and answer the following questions:

  a. What did David desire to do throughout the seasons/days of his life?

  b. What specific time/season did David refer to in verse 5?

  c. What did David say God would do during that specific time/season?

 8. Read Psalm 31:9–15 and answer the following questions:

  a. As you read this passage, what type of season was David experiencing?

  b. According to verse 15a, what did David know about God?

  c. What was David's response to this season of his life?

9. In Acts 17 you'll find an account of Paul's address to the Greek philosophers and religious leaders of Athens. Please read Acts 17:22–28, then answer the following questions:

   a. According to verse 26, what did God specifically determine regarding all mankind? Please explain your answer.

   b. According to verse 27, what was God's desire for mankind?

10. Based on what you have seen today:

   a. Who ultimately determines the literal and figurative times and seasons of life?

   b. How should we respond to the seasons of life?

Insights

11. What about you? What season are you currently experiencing in your life, and how are you responding? What insight has the Holy Spirit given you for your own personal life?

Thy word is a lamp to my feet, and a light to my path.
Psalm 119:105

The unfolding of Thy words gives light.
Psalm 119:130

_____

_____

_____

_____

_____

_____

_____

_____

There is a **Season**

Day Two

Yesterday we learned God is sovereign over every season. And we learned these seasons include literal seasons as well as figurative ones. Today you will study Ecclesiastes 3:2–8 and learn more about the seasons of life.

1. Begin your study today in prayer. Commit to observe and obey what you study from God's Word just as the psalmist did in Psalm 119:15.

I will meditate on Thy precepts,
and regard Thy ways. Psalm 119:15

2. Read Ecclesiastes 3:2–8, noticing the repeated pattern Solomon used in this passage. Explain this pattern and why Solomon used it.

3. Using Ecclesiastes 3:2–8, fill in the chart you see on the next few pages by:
   a. Listing the specific seasons in the shaded boxes using words from the verse.
   b. Describing some of the things that specific season would include and any personal experiences you may have had regarding that particular season.

NOTE: You may want to read these verses from several Bible translations in order to gain broader insight. If you have access to Bible study tools such as word study books, commentaries, etc., you may also use them. Or go online and use Bible commentary sources (such as www.bibleclassics.com, www. biblegateway.com, and www.studylight.org) to research this passage.

In order to help you begin, the first seasons (from Ecclesiastes 3:2a) have been completed by Laurie for you.

THE SEASONS OF LIFE—ECCLESIASTES 3:2–8

A TIME TO…	AND A TIME TO…
1. v. 2a Give Birth	**1. v. 2a Die**
There is a time in life to experience the joys of childbirth and the changes and responsibilities giving birth to a child brings into our lives. When I gave birth, not only did a new life begin, but I began a new season in my life as a mother. I must also face the fact my childbearing days begin and end in God's time.	There is a time in life to experience death and the resulting changes death always brings. I must accept God's sovereign decision in appointing this difficult time. Went to a funeral this past week for a young man who had a young wife and small children. Sometimes it is very hard to accept the truth of this verse.

A Time to...

2. v. 2b

_____
_____
_____
_____
_____

3. v. 3a

_____
_____
_____
_____
_____
_____

4. v. 3b

_____
_____
_____
_____
_____
_____

5. v. 4a

_____
_____
_____
_____
_____

6. v. 4b

_____
_____
_____
_____

And a Time to...

2. v. 2b

_____
_____
_____
_____
_____

3. v. 3a

_____
_____
_____
_____
_____
_____

4. v. 3b

_____
_____
_____
_____
_____
_____

5. v. 4a

_____
_____
_____
_____
_____

6. v. 4b

_____
_____
_____
_____

There is a **Season**

A Time to…	And a Time to…
7. v. 5a	**7. v. 5a**
8. v. 5b	**8. v. 5b**
9. v. 6a	**9. v. 6a**
10. v. 6b	**10. v. 6b**
11. v. 7a	**11. v. 7a**

A TIME TO…	AND A TIME TO…
12. v. 7b	**12. v. 7b**
_____	_____
_____	_____
_____	_____
_____	_____
_____	_____
13. v. 8a	**13. v. 8a**
_____	_____
_____	_____
_____	_____
_____	_____
_____	_____
_____	_____
14. v. 8b	**14. v. 8b**
_____	_____
_____	_____
_____	_____
_____	_____
_____	_____
_____	_____

Insights

4. Spend a few moments reflecting on the insights God has given you as you have meditated on Ecclesiastes 3:2–8. In the space provided below, explain the most important insight He has shown you through this passage and how you feel led to apply it to your life.

Thy word is a lamp to my feet, and a light to my path.
Psalm 119:105

The unfolding of Thy words gives light.
Psalm 119:130

_____

_____

_____

_____

_____

_____

_____

There is a **Season**

Days Three and Four

1. Begin your study for the next two days in prayer just like you always do. Claim the words from Psalm 119:24 as your own as you seek counsel from His Word.

Thy testimonies also are my delight;
they are my counselors. Psalm 119:24

This week as we have studied the seasons of life, we have seen two primary principles:

1) God is sovereign over the seasons of life. He ultimately determines and appoints each of them.

2) These seasons include not only the literal earthly seasons such as spring and summer, but they also include the various seasons of life which we saw in Ecclesiastes 3:2–8. Ecclesiastes very clearly shows us that our lives consist of a series of ever-changing experiences and circumstances.

For the next two days, you will be looking at the seasons of life from a very female perspective. As women, our lives are a succession of many physiological seasons. Beginning with puberty and periods, women progress into PMS, pregnancy and young motherhood, pre-menopause, menopause, and post-menopause. It is enormously important that we understand how each of these physiological seasons affects us not only physically, but emotionally and spiritually as well.

Your homework assignment for the next two days will be a little different than usual. It has been divided into two parts, and you need to complete both. You may do either Part I or Part II first.

Part I will be a brief study of the book of Ruth. This little book is only four chapters long. It is a beautiful story about two women at two very different physiological seasons of their lives.

Part II will simply be an evaluation of the physiological seasons of your own life. Please be sure to complete this part of your assignment. If you are doing this study with a group, this assignment will be a significant part of your group discussion.

Go ahead and get started. These two days of study will be enjoyable and practical.

PART I

Use your Bible to read through the entire book of Ruth. After you have finished, answer the following questions:

1. Note what you learned about Naomi from Ruth 1:1–5. What is her approximate age/stage in life? What seasons of circumstances does she experience in these verses?

2. In her grief, what decision did Naomi make in verse 6?

3. Note what you learned about Ruth from Ruth 1:4–18. What is her approximate age/stage in life? What seasons of circumstances does she experience in these verses?

4. How does Naomi feel about her life and future and (based on Ruth 1:11–13) how does her physiological season affect her outlook?

5. According to Ruth 1:19–22, what is Naomi's attitude toward her life and toward God during this season in her life?

6. In Ruth 1:22, there is a reference to the literal season in which this story occurs. What season was it?

7. According to Ruth 2:2–3, what was Ruth's role and attitude during this season in her life?

8. Where did God sovereignly lead Ruth during this season according to Ruth 2:3?

9. According to Ruth 2:4–12, what was Ruth's reputation during this season in her life? What did Boaz know about her?

10. During this uncertain season in Ruth's and Naomi's life, in what ways did God provide for them based on Ruth 2?

11. In Ruth 2:23, there is a reference to the change in season. Note the season change, and how it would have affected Ruth and Naomi.

12. How did God use Naomi in an instrumental way in Ruth's life in Ruth 3? Do you think Ruth would have done what she did on her own?

13. In Ruth 2, we see the strength and capabilities of Ruth's physiological season of life. What kind of strength did she have at that season of her life, and how did it benefit Naomi?

14. In Ruth 3, we see a different type of strength and capability in Naomi during that particular physiological season of her life. What type of strength did Naomi have and how did it benefit Ruth?

15. Ruth 4 is the account of Boaz marrying Ruth. Read Ruth 4:13–17 and describe how Ruth and Naomi's lives (and attitudes) have radically changed since Ruth 1.

16. Approximately how much time passed between Ruth 1:22 (when Ruth and Naomi arrived in Bethlehem) and Ruth 4:13 (when Ruth became a mother and Naomi became a grandmother)? How does this correlate with what you know about seasons?

17. What principles did you learn about the seasons of life from the book of Ruth?

18. What did you learn about God from the book of Ruth?

PART II

In this assignment, you will be writing a physiological evaluation of the seasons of your life. Because of the unique way God has created us as women, we have some very distinct physiological seasons in our lives. Each of these seasons can profoundly impact our physical, emotional, and spiritual lives (PMS can sometimes make you doubt your salvation!). The following chart lists five of the physiological seasons of a woman's life. Beside each season are six boxes in which you will write your responses to the following topics:

Greatest Joys/Greatest Challenges—List those things that give/gave you the greatest joy/challenge in that particular season.

Greatest Strengths/Greatest Weaknesses—List the greatest strengths/greatest weaknesses you possess/possessed in that season.

Outlook & Attitude—Describe your general outlook and attitude toward life during that season. Example: optimistic, pessimistic, happy, sad, idealistic, realistic, etc.

New Opportunities—Describe those things you discovered or were able to do in that season. These would be things you had not been able to do or to discover in previous seasons.

NOTE: Please complete every box even though you may not have experienced all of these seasons yet. If you get to a season you haven't experienced, simply describe what you think that season will be like for you.

The Seasons of Life

There is a Season	Greatest Joys	Greatest Challenges	Greatest Strengths	Greatest Weaknesses	Outlook & Attitude	New Opportunities
Season 1 **Age 20–35** *Periods, Pregnancy and PMS*						
Season 2 **Age 35–45** *Mid-Life*						
Season 3 **Age 45–55** *Pre-Menopause*						
Season 4 **Age 55–65** *Menopause*						
Season 5 **Age 65+** *Post-menopause*						

2. To conclude these two days of study, note any insights the Lord has given you as you have studied and evaluated the physiological seasons of life.

Thy word is a lamp to my feet, and a light to my path.
Psalm 119:105

The unfolding of Thy words gives light.
Psalm 119:130

_____

_____

_____

_____

_____

Day Five

1. Take a few moments to spend in prayer before you begin your study. Ask Him to give you the kind of heart described in Psalm 119:10.

   With all my heart I have sought Thee; do not let me wander from Thy commandments. Psalm 119:10

   Because you have worked so hard this week, your final day of study will be light.

2. There is another aspect of the seasons of life we need to examine. As Christians, we experience *spiritual seasons* in our lives. Use your Bible to read the following cross references. Then, describe the spiritual season referred to in that verse and any insights or instructions you may see regarding that particular season.

   a.   1 Peter 2:2

   b.   1 Corinthians 3:1–3

   c.   Hebrews 5:12–14

   d.   1 Peter 1:6–7 (**NOTE: The KJV translates the first part of verse 6 as "Wherein ye greatly rejoice, though now for a season…"**)

   e.   Galatians 6:9–10

3. One final question: how would you describe your own current spiritual season?

4. Conclude your studies this week by journaling as you did last week. Reflect upon what the Lord has revealed to you this week and the ways you see Him working in your life. Journal your thoughts by completing the sentences provided.

My Journal

THIS WEEK THE LORD...

_____

_____

_____

_____

_____

_____

_____

_____

AS A RESULT, I...

_____

_____

_____

_____

_____

_____

_____

_____

Our week has been full and somewhat introspective as we've looked at life's seasons from many different perspectives. What I hope you've seen very clearly thus far is the awesome sovereignty of Almighty God over every season: the literal earthly seasons, the seasons of our circumstances and life experiences, the physiological seasons of our lives as women, and our spiritual seasons.

I believe God wants us to say as David did, "But as for me, I trust in Thee, O Lord, I say, 'Thou art my God.' My times are in thy hands." (Psalm 31:14–15). I pray, dear sister, that God would bring you to that same point of submission to His sovereignty no matter what season of life you're currently experiencing. For only then will you discover true contentment.

The Seasons of Life

I. As Christian women, we will experience many different types of seasons which will

simultaneously _____ to affect us in many _____

and _____ ways throughout our lifetime.

    A. _____ Seasons: caused by _____ and our

       reproductive system including…

       _____

       _____

       _____

       _____

       _____

    B. Seasons of _____ and Life _____ including…

       _____   _____

       _____   _____

       _____   _____

    C. _____ Seasons: including…

       _____

       _____

       _____

II. As Christian women, our faith in God and His Word must always be the _____

_____ in determining how we live and respond to *every* season of our lives.

III. Walking by Faith in Every Season—*Ruth 1–4*

    A. Two Women Who Walked by Faith:

	Naomi	Ruth
Physical	_____	_____
Circumstances	_____	_____
Spiritual	_____	_____

Listening Guide—Week Two

B. In Seasons of...

1. Extreme and _____ circumstances, God is pleased by our

   _____, "_____ _____" of faith. *Ruth 1*

   We may struggle with

   _____   _____

   _____   _____

   _____

2. _____, day-to-day activities, God is pleased by _____,

   obedient steps of faith. *Ruth 2*

   These simple steps will:

   _____

   _____

3. _____, God may require us to take a _____ of

   _____ in order to follow Him. *Ruth 3*

   _____

   _____

4. _____, we will experience God's _____ of faith. *Ruth 4*

   _____

   _____

   _____

The Seasons of David's Life

Almost twenty-five years ago, our family moved to Amarillo, Texas, where my husband, Bill, had accepted the call to become the minister of music at a wonderful church. Bill and I are lifelong Texans, but until then, we'd always lived in the central part of the state in the Dallas/Fort Worth area. We arrived in Amarillo with our two young sons in early September 1984, and I will never forget what I saw the very first week we were there. Early one morning as I stepped outside, I was utterly astonished to see a very strange phenomenon: September snow! Tiny white flurries swirled all around me. Instantly I realized that, although we were still in Texas, we now lived in a very different place.

The winters in Amarillo were long, hard, cold and snowy—very unlike any I had ever experienced before. But as I look back now, even the coldest, most bitter and challenging winters we spent there were surpassed by the warm, extended season of spring I experienced in my own life. During those few brief years among the warm, loving West Texas people of our church, I blossomed and thrived. Amarillo was where I first became involved in Bible study and learned to really study God's Word. Amarillo was where I first discovered my spiritual gift as some older women (my Bible study teacher, Georgia Kerns, and my pastor's wife, Glenda Coffey) encouraged and mentored me. In Amarillo my boys were still very small, and during their naptime each day I enjoyed long, uninterrupted quiet times with God. For me, Amarillo was a season of spring: a warm, mild season of spiritual and personal growth.

I share that memory with you because I want you to begin to see how *the seasons of our lives often mirror the seasons of nature*. Let me clarify and explain this a little further. When life is joyous and peaceful, when we feel bright and alive, when most everything in our life seems warm and wonderful, we experience a kind of **springtime**. When life heats up and we find ourselves seizing new opportunities and responsibilities resulting in a more accelerated way of life, we often experience a kind of **summer**. When the winds of change begin to blow through our lives leaving us feeling unsteady, uneasy, and unsure, we experience a kind of **autumn**. And when we face prolonged challenges and difficult circumstances, when we feel isolated and alone, when life seems cold and hard, we experience a kind of **winter** in our lives. Each season is distinctly different and includes its own unique blessings and challenges.

For the next two weeks you will be studying one of the most well-documented characters in the Old Testament: David. You will meet him in his youth, and you will follow him through a succession of the seasons of his life into his adulthood. You will read the historical narratives about him from the pages of scripture, but you'll also glimpse into David's own personal diary—the Psalms—where he bares his soul through his prayers to God.

One of the primary reasons God recorded the details of David's life (the good, the bad, and the ugly) is so we would learn from David's successes and failures. In the coming weeks, you will be evaluating the seasons of your own life with the same purpose in mind: to gain insight and wisdom from your own past successes and failures that will enable you to wisely navigate through future seasons to come.

Almost twenty-five years have passed since I enjoyed that glorious springtime in Amarillo. Little did I know how abruptly spring would end and how quickly winter would come. But God knew. And the One who is sovereign over all of the seasons of our lives would use the things He planted in my life during spring to prepare and sustain me during the cold winter that He knew lay ahead for me. Dear sister, I firmly believe God wants to do the same thing in your life through this study. Study well this week. Allow Him to plant His Word deep within your heart so that it will prepare and sustain through warm seasons, cold seasons, dry seasons, rainy seasons…well, you get the idea!

To every thing there is a season…a time to plant, and a time to pluck up that which is planted. Ecclesiastes 3:1–2 (KJV)

The grass withers, the flower fades, but the word of our God stands forever. Isaiah 40:8

This week we will be studying the seasons of David's life. In no way will we be able to cover every season of David's entire life. Instead, we will limit our focus this week to observing and studying the first half of David's life. **The primary goals of this week's study are that you would:**

1. Identify and understand which seasons (spring, summer, autumn, or winter as defined on the previous page) David's life seems to mirror most at various points in his journey.

2. Identify and understand the ways in which God faithfully works through and sovereignly uses each season in David's life.

3. Identify the recurring characteristics David displays in his life as he responds to each season.

4. Identify on a personal, emotional, and spiritual level with David as you seek to put yourself in his "sandals" as you read about the seasons of his life.

As always, the ultimate goal of all Bible study is that you would grow in your own spiritual life and relationship with God. Be sensitive to the prompting of His Spirit as He leads you to apply the truths you study this week to your life.

Day One

1. Before you do anything else, take a few minutes to pray and confess your need to be tutored and taught by the Holy Spirit. Let today's scripture from Psalm 119 be your guide as you pray.

Open my eyes, that I may behold wonderful things from Thy law. Psalm 119:18

2. Keeping in mind the goals listed in the introduction to this lesson, observe carefully and read 1 Samuel 16:1–13.

3. According to 1 Samuel 16, briefly note your answers to the following questions:

   a. Who is the king of Israel, and what does God think about him in verse 1?

   b. What did God instruct Samuel to do in verses 1–3?

   c. According to verses 6–7, what were God's primary criteria for selecting the next king?

   d. While seven of Jesse's sons passed by Samuel, where was David and what was his position and rank within his family?

   e. Given David's position and rank, and given the fact that he was obviously left out of this auspicious occasion, how was David most likely regarded by his family?

   f. What did God see in David that his family did not?

   g. According to verses 7, and 12–13, what did you learn about David's outward and inward characteristics, and what happened to him that day that would change his life from that time forward?

   h. Put yourself in David's "sandals," and describe what his lifestyle was probably like prior to verse 12.

4. Some scholars believe Psalm 8 and Psalm 19 were written during the season of David's life you have just read about in 1 Samuel 16. Read both of these Psalms.

   a. Briefly summarize some of the topics and themes of these two Psalms.

b. How do their topics and themes reflect the viewpoint of a shepherd?

c. What does Psalm 19:7–11 reveal about David's own spiritual life during this season of his life?

d. What were David's prayer requests and concerns in Psalm 19:12–14 and what do they reveal about his heart?

5. Considering everything you have just read, what season does David's life most parallel? **(NOTE: if necessary, please refer to the definitions of each season on page 39.)** Circle one:

> *winter*   *spring*   *summer*   *autumn*

Explain your answer and the specific ways David's life parallels the season you have circled.

6. Briefly share your own thoughts on the ways God may have used and worked through this season in David's life.

Thy word is a lamp to my feet, and a light to my path.
Psalm 119:105

The unfolding of Thy words gives light.
Psalm 119:130

7. Finally, what insight has the Lord shown you today for your own personal application? As you've studied David's life thus far, how has it affected you spiritually?

_____

_____

_____

_____

_____

_____

_____

Day Two

1. Perhaps you are experiencing a dry season in your spiritual life. Sometimes we may feel God is distant because we cannot seem to connect with Him even when we pray and even when we know there is no personal sin blocking our fellowship with Him. In truth, however, seasons change but God does not. He promises "He will never (leave) us," and He will always be our "helper" (Hebrews 13:5–6). If you are experiencing a spiritual "dry spell," use today's scripture to cry out to God. By faith, believe He hears. By faith, believe He will soon answer and revive you.

My soul cleaves to the dust; Revive me
according to Thy word. Psalm 119:25

2. David's life changes dramatically beginning in 1 Samuel 16:14. Keeping in mind the goals listed in the introduction to this lesson, observe carefully and read 1 Samuel 16:14–23.

   a. Briefly summarize King Saul's problem and the solution to his problem.

   b. Using verse 18, list David's attributes.

   c. According to verses 21–23, what was David's ministry to Saul and how did Saul feel about David?

   d. Put yourself in David's "sandals," and describe what his lifestyle was like in the king's courts and how it would have been different from his previous lifestyle as a shepherd.

3. In 1 Samuel 17, we learn Saul and his army are at war with the Philistines. Saul is no longer at the palace, but on the battlefield near Socoh. David is no longer at the palace either. He is dividing his time between serving Saul and tending his father's flock (verse 15). In other words, David is doing two things at once. The Philistine giant, Goliath, has been taunting the army of Israel for forty days. David arrives at the battlefield at that same time, and you're probably familiar with the rest of the story as David defeats Goliath with a single shot from his sling. Just prior to David's showdown with Goliath, Saul and David meet together. Their conversation is recorded in 1 Samuel 17:32–37. Read that passage, then answer the following questions:

    a.   How had David's season as a shepherd prepared him for battle against Goliath?

    b.   Why is David so confident he can defeat Goliath?

4. As David meets Goliath, he courageously preaches a sermon of sorts to the pagan giant before he slays him. Read this account in 1 Samuel 17:45–50, and briefly explain David's purpose or motive in defeating Goliath. Also, note what it reveals about David's heart and his relationship with God.

5. Several life-changing things happen to David after his defeat of Goliath. Read 1 Samuel 18:1–5, and note the ways David's life and responsibilities again change.

6. Considering everything you have just read, what season does David's life most parallel? **(NOTE: if necessary, please refer to the definitions of each season on page 39.)** Circle one:

winter   spring   summer   autumn

Explain your answer and the specific ways David's life parallels the season you have circled.

7. Briefly share your own thoughts on the ways God may have used and worked through this season in David's life to prepare him for the seasons ahead.

Insights

8. Finally, what insight has the Lord shown you today for your own personal application? What characteristics in David's life do you think God desires to develop in your life?

_____

_____

_____

_____

_____

_____

Thy word is a lamp to my feet, and a light to my path.
Psalm 119:105

The unfolding of Thy words gives light.
Psalm 119:130

Day Three

1. God blesses and changes the lives of those (like you) who choose to study His Word. Have you noticed that when you take time to read and study the Bible consistently, you also find yourself thinking about the Word more consistently? This kind of thinking is true, biblical meditation. And consistent meditation results in a renewed mind. And a renewed mind results in a transformed life—hallelujah! As you begin your study today, ask God to allow His Word to radically renew your mind and to totally transform your life. That's a prayer He's going to want to answer!

Pray

Make me understand the way of Thy precepts, so I will meditate on Thy wonders. Psalm 119:27

There is a Season

2. In our study today, we'll see the seasons of David's life change again. David's "Number 1 Fan," King Saul, becomes his "Number 1 Enemy." It is a very turbulent time in David's life. Read 1 Samuel 18:6–19:24, and answer the following questions:

   a. What did Saul unsuccessfully try to do to David time and time again?

   b. What were David's activities and responsibilities during this time in his life.

   c. According to 1 Samuel 18:12, 15, 28–29, and 19:4–7, what did even unstable King Saul recognize about David?

   d. How did David respond in his attitude and service toward Saul?

3. Some scholars believe David wrote Psalm 59 at the same time the events in 1 Samuel 19 occurred. Read this Psalm, and briefly summarize David's prayer requests, what he believes about God, and the active evidences of faith you observe in his life.

4. Considering everything you have just read, what season does David's life most parallel? **(NOTE: if necessary, please refer to the definitions of each season on page 39.)** Circle one:

   winter   *spring*   *summer*   *autumn*

   Explain your answer and the specific ways David's life parallels the season you've circled.

5. Briefly share you own thoughts on the ways God may have used and worked through this season of David's life to teach and prepare him for the future.

6. As you conclude your study time, what insight has the Lord shown you today for your own personal application? How do you usually respond during the turbulent seasons of your life? How has the Holy Spirit spoken to you through David's example?

Thy word is a lamp to my feet, and a light to my path.
Psalm 119:105

The unfolding of Thy words gives light.
Psalm 119:130

_____

_____

_____

_____

_____

_____

_____

Day Four

1. Have you been impressed by David's faith and deep love for God as you have studied his life this week? God describes David as "a man after (His) own heart," (1 Samuel 13:14). Psalm 119:32 reveals God can enlarge our heart for Him when we diligently seek to keep His Word. Before you hastily begin to do your homework, drop to your knees and prayerfully commit to obey the scriptures you will study today. Then, ask God to enlarge your heart and your passion for Him.

I shall run the way of Thy commandments, for Thou wilt enlarge my heart. Psalm 119:32

2. Yesterday you studied a season of great distress in David's life. Today you will follow David to a field not far from the king's palace where the seasons of his life will change again.

    a. After David fully realizes that Saul will kill him if he returns to the palace, David secretly meets with Jonathan to say good bye. Read 1 Samuel 20:41–42 and note below what you learn about David's emotional state.

    b.   Put yourself in David's "sandals," and consider the past few years of his life: from the time he was an unknown shepherd, then a well-known hero, the best friend of Saul's son, the powerful commander of Israel's army, and the son-in-law of the king. Describe how all of that would have affected and impacted David's emotions at this time. Also, list any questions you would ask God if you were in David's position.

3.   David will live his life as a fugitive for approximately ten years until Saul finally dies. The following passages chronicle only a few years of this season of David's life. Read each passage, then answer the following questions.

    a.   1 Samuel 21:1–9—Where is David? What provisions and weapons did David take with him when he left Jerusalem? How does God provide for David?

    b.   1 Samuel 21:10–15—Where is David now? Why does David disguise his sanity before Achish? (This has to be a very low point in David's life.)

    c.   1 Samuel 22:1–2—Where is David now? How does God provide for David?

    d.   1 Samuel 22:3–5—Where is David now? David's family members are in peril, too, so David seeks their protection. When he speaks to the king of Moab, we learn David is uncertain about something else. Of what is David uncertain?

4.   In 1 Samuel 23, David is in the Philistine town of Keilah where God has allowed David and his men to be the victors of a battle. Meanwhile, Saul has slain the priest, Ahimelech, in Nob because of Ahimelech's past assistance to David. Ahimelech's son, Abiathar, then escapes from Saul and flees to Keilah to seek David's protection. Read 1 Samuel 23:6–14 and answer the following questions:

    a.   What is David's response to Saul's threat in verses 9–13?

    b.   According to verse 13, how many men are now following David?

c.   According to verse 14, how persistent was Saul's passion to kill David?

d.   According to verse 14, who is ultimately always in control of even the most difficult times of our lives?

5.   Read 1 Samuel 23:15–29, then answer the following questions:

a.   How was God at work in David's life in verses 15–18? Who did God use and how did He use him in this season of David's life?

The passage above contains Jonathan's final words to his dear friend, David. They would never meet again during their lifetimes (although I certainly believe they're enjoying one another's company right now). Next week we'll look at Jonathan, but I wanted you to just pause a moment and re-read verses 15–18. Note the significance of Jonathan's last words to David, the character of Jonathan, and the goodness of God.

b.   Saul continues to pursue David in verses 19–29. What happened to David and his men in verses 25–26? How close was David to death?

c.   The first word in verse 27 is a wonderful little word. That word is "but." What is the significance of that word, and what does it reveal about the way God was at work?

6.   Considering everything you have just read today, what season does David's life most parallel? **(NOTE: if necessary, please refer to the definitions of each season on page 39.)** Circle one:

winter   spring   summer   autumn

Explain your answer and the specific ways David's life parallels the season you have circled.

7. Briefly share your own thoughts on the ways God may have used and worked through this season in David's life to teach and prepare him for the future.

Thy word is a lamp to my feet, and a light to my path.
Psalm 119:105

The unfolding of Thy words gives light.
Psalm 119:130

8. As you conclude your study time, what insight has the Lord shown you today for your own personal application? What did you learn about God that you can apply in your own walk with Him?

_____

_____

_____

_____

_____

_____

_____

_____

Day Five

Today's homework will be a little different. We have completed our overview of the seasons of David's life. For our final day of study, you will be looking at a Psalm David wrote during a dark season in his life. You will see his honest description of his circumstances, but you will also see his deep faith. Finally, you will see David state something that is remarkable—and downright stunning—in light of his circumstances. After you have studied that Psalm, you will be doing a brief evaluation of the seasons of your own life.

1. As usual, spend a few moments in prayer before you begin your homework. Tell God that Psalm 119:34 is the desire of your heart.

> *Give me understanding, that I may observe Thy Law,*
> *And keep it with all my heart.* Psalm 119:34

2. Read Psalm 17, then answer the questions listed below:
   a. According to verse 3, what did God do in David's life during this difficult season?

b. How does David describe his own spiritual life and behavior in verses 1 and 3–6? How is he responding to this challenging season?

c. According to verses 6–7, what does David know about God?

d. According to verses 9–12, what are David's circumstances?

e. In verse 15, before David lies down to sleep, what does he state about himself even in the midst of his fearful circumstances.

3. In Lesson 1, we looked at two very different people: the Proverbs 31 woman and Solomon from Ecclesiastes 1. We also learned that the word "content" means to be satisfied. Proverbs 31 describes a woman whose life epitomizes contentment and satisfaction in life. Ecclesiastes 1 describes Solomon's life as vain and dissatisfying. Now we see David's outlook on life during this trying season in his life. What does Psalm 17:15 reveal about contentment and satisfaction in life?

One of the goals of this study is that you learn how to experience joy, meaning, and contentment (satisfaction) in every season of life. In the weeks ahead, we will focus more on the "how tos" of contentment. But for now, I want you to recognize that David is a wonderful example of contentment even in the midst of a very desperate season in his life.

4. As you have studied the seasons of David's life this week, you have probably recalled some of your own personal seasons and circumstances. Using the chart on the following pages, briefly describe some of the seasons of your life.

INSTRUCTIONS FOR "SEASONS CHART"

Each section of the chart represents a different season of your life. In each section, briefly describe an illustration from your life in which your circumstances paralleled that season.

In your description, include:
- How you responded to your circumstances,
- How God used that season in your life,
- What you learned about God as a result of that season, and
- What you learned about yourself as a result of that season.

NOTE: Limit yourself to one or two illustrations for each season.

Seasons Chart

SPRING	_____ _____ _____ _____ _____ _____ _____ _____ _____ _____ _____ _____ _____ _____ _____ _____
FALL	_____ _____ _____ _____ _____ _____ _____ _____ _____ _____ _____ _____ _____ _____ _____ _____

SUMMER

WINTER

5. Close your time of study this week by journaling, reflecting upon what God has shown you this week and the ways you sense He is working in your life in this current season.

My Journal

THIS WEEK THE LORD...

_____

_____

_____

_____

_____

_____

_____

_____

_____

_____

AS A RESULT, I...

_____

_____

_____

_____

_____

_____

_____

_____

_____

_____

_____

My sister, our lives truly are a succession of seasons. I hope you've come to the place where you are able to recognize the Father's hand in each season of your life. But may we not simply recognize Him. May we also be like David and fully embrace Him through every spring, summer, fall, and winter of our lives.

The Seasons of David's Life

I. What is a season?

Definition: Season[4] = Hebrew "_____" which means:

- time
- the right time
- the proper time
- may be either short-lived or a longer time
- the (favorable or unfavorable) events in life
- in the plural it means circumstances, courses of time, occurrences, and events

II. What have we learned about seasons thus far?

A. God is sovereign over the seasons of our lives. *Ecc. 3:1–8*

B. As Christian women, we will experience many different types of seasons which will simultaneously combine to affect us in many positive and negative ways throughout our lifetime.

C. As Christian women, our faith in God and His Word must always be the primary factor in determining how we live and respond to every season of our lives.

III. What other principles should we understand about the seasons of life?

The seasons of our lives will

A. Be determined primarily by the _____ and _____ of our lives.

B. _____ throughout our lives and will _____ in their length.

C. Often _____ the characteristics of the seasons of nature.

D. Not always correlate with our physical _____ or _____ in life.

E. Not always _____ and _____ one another in a consistent order as the seasons of nature do.

IV. Evaluating the Seasons—*1 Samuel 16–20*

A. _____—*1 Sam. 16:11–13*

  1. Evidence of Spring:

     - season of _____ / _____.
     - season of _____ _____ / _____.
     - season of spiritual _____ and "_____."
     - season of growing _____ with God.

  2. Essentials for Spring:

     - seek Him _____. *Matt. 6:33*
     - seek Him in extended _____ and _____. *Psalm 23:2-3, 46:10*
     - seek _____ _____ through His Word. *1 Pet. 2:2*

B. _____*—1 Sam. 16:14–21, 17:17–18:4*

  1. Evidence of Summer:

   • season of new _____.

   • season of increased _____.

   • season of spiritual _____.

   • season of _____.

  2. Essentials for Summer:

   • guard your _____. *2 Cor. 11:3*

   • guard your _____. *John 7:18, 1 Cor. 10:31*

   • guard your _____. *John 15:15*

C. _____*—1 Sam. 18:5–11*

  1. Evidence of Autumn:

   • season of _____.

   • season of _____ / _____ / _____.

   • season of new/unexpected _____.

   • season of _____.

  2. Essentials for Autumn:

   • seek and _____ in _____. *Eph. 5:15–18, Jas. 1:5, 3:17*

   • seek _____ _____. *1 Sam. 19:18*

   • seek God through:

    a. _____ to His Will, and

    b. for _____ in your circumstances. *Ps. 9:9–10, Prov. 18:10*

D. _____*—1 Sam. 20:41–42*

  1. Evidence of Winter:

   • season of _____ / _____.

   • season of _____ / _____.

   • season of _____ _____.

   • season of _____.

  2. Essentials for Winter:

   • _____ the loss. *Ecc. 3:4 and 6*

   • _____ _____ to God: PRAY. *Ps. 142*

    – _____

    – _____

    – _____

    – _____

   • _____ _____. *v. 7*

   • offer God the _____ of _____. *Is. 61:3, Heb. 13:15*

In Every Season: Godsends and Giants

How do you normally respond when someone says, "I have some good news and some bad news. Which one do you want to hear first?" Personally, I think your response may depend upon your temperament. For example, as one who is melancholy in temperament, I usually want to hear the bad news first because bad news is the kind of news I usually expect (we "melancholies" tend to be a pretty negative bunch). That way, when the good news is delivered, it's not only a surprise, but it also leaves me in a positive frame of mind which I usually (OK, almost always) need. (Note to my fellow "melancholies" out there: in the weeks ahead I have some really good news for you, so please—hang in there!)

This week's lesson is a little like that "good news/bad news" dilemma. But I've decided to rise above my melancholy tendencies and give you the good news first. The good news is that this week you will be studying a tremendously encouraging topic. It deals with relationships and as women, relationships are very high on our list of priorities. In the first part of your homework, you will be looking at some of David's relationships. You'll study some of the people God sent into his life and used in significant ways. I call these people "Godsends," and I'll give you my definition a little further on.

But (no surprise to you "melancholies"), here's the bad news: this week you're also going to study a tremendously challenging topic. The last part of your homework will be a study about giants—both the literal and figurative kind. David faced his share of both literal (Goliath) and figurative (sin, discouragement, sorrow, etc.) giants. So will we—but thankfully, not the 9-foot, 6-toed variety!

I have two reasons for giving you the good news first. Let's be honest. I know some weeks it's just downright hard to complete your homework. This brings me to my first reason for giving you the "good news" part of your homework first. By giving you the pleasant, enjoyable topic to study first, I'm hoping time will just fly as you delve into your homework leaving you with more than enough time to complete the entire assignment—even the more challenging topic in the final part of the lesson.

Some of you are doing this study with a group, which brings me to my second reason for giving you the "good news" portion of your homework first. You see, I know about the "snowball effect." Allow me to explain. Sometimes (especially when our Bible study homework is challenging), we simply don't complete it. That's when the snowball begins to roll for those of you in a group study. The following is a detailed description of how it continues to roll, and roll, and roll:

The Snowball Effect
Or
**"I wonder what happened to that really nice woman
who used to be in our Bible study group?"**

- You don't finish your Bible study homework.
- You become discouraged and frustrated with yourself.
- You start to think about how uncomfortable you're going to feel sitting in your group with blank workbook pages.

- You consider skipping class that week.
- You think a little harder and soon discover there are lots of good reasons to skip class that week.
- You skip class.
- You miss the group share time which usually encourages you to attend the next session.
- You feel twice as discouraged because not only did you not complete your homework, you also skipped class.
- You begin to think maybe it's just "not God's timing" for you to do the study.
- You think a little harder and soon discover there are lots of good reasons to quit the study.
- You quit the study.

That, my sister, is the "snowball effect"—and it's not just the melancholy group members who experience it!

All of this provides me with a perfect opportunity to encourage you. If you're doing this study with a group, please don't let an incomplete lesson keep you from attending class. God will bless the time you did spend in His Word, and you will reap greater blessings from keeping your commitment to your group. If you're doing this study on your own, persevere. Even though you may not be progressing as quickly through the homework as you had planned, God will bless your diligence and reward your commitment to study His Word.

This week you will see both the Godsends and giants in David's life. Now, let me define what I mean by Godsends and giants by giving you two principles you will clearly see in this lesson:

1) In every season of your life, God will faithfully bring significant and influential people into your life. He will use these special people to impact your life for His divine purposes. I call these people "Godsends."

2) In every season of your life, God will sovereignly allow you to face difficult circumstances, difficult people, trials, and testings in order to mature your faith and increase your dependence upon Him. I call these "giants."

Godsends: the good news in our lesson this week. Giants: the bad news—or is it really? I'll close for now with a familiar verse and let *you* decide.

And we know that God causes all things to work together for good to those who love God, to those who are called according to His purpose. Romans 8:28

Days One — Three

1. Prepare your heart for these three days of study by spending a few moments each day in prayer. You have been given three scriptures from Psalm 119 to help you begin your prayer time as you prepare your heart to receive the Word. Use a different scripture each day.

> *Teach me, O Lord, the way of Thy statutes,*
> *and I shall observe it to the end.* Psalm 119:33
>
> *Establish Thy word to Thy servant, as that*
> *which produces reverence for Thee.* Psalm 119:38
>
> *May Thy lovingkindness also come to me, O Lord,*
> *Thy salvation according to Thy word.* Psalm 119:41

2. Before you begin to study the Godsends in David's life, take a few moments to read the following cross references and briefly note the ways God uses other people in our lives and desires to use us in the lives of others.

   a.   Job 6:14

   b.   Proverbs 17:17

   c.   Proverbs 27:6

   d.   Proverbs 27:9

   e.   2 Corinthians 1:3–4

   f.   Galatians 6:1–2

   g.   1 Thessalonians 5:14

THE GODSENDS IN DAVID'S LIFE

You will now begin a three-day study of some of the Godsends in David's life. On the following pages, you will see charts with the names of five influential men (Godsends) God used to impact David's life. ***From these five men, prayerfully choose <u>three</u> to study. Plan to study one per day.***

You will begin your study each day by reading the scripture study provided for the Godsend you have chosen. Brief commentary is given with each passage to help you in understanding the scriptural context. Read each passage, then answer the questions on the chart. As you complete each chart, please keep the following in mind:

1. The significance of that Godsend in light of the particular season in which they influenced David's life.

2. The insights you learned from the cross references you studied at the beginning of this lesson.

3. The definition of a Godsend given in the introduction to this week's lesson.

Some of these Godsends may be more familiar to you than others are, but don't let that influence your choice as you determine which ones to study. Personally, my favorite from these five men is probably the one who is the least known: Hushai. I think he's my favorite simply because he was someone I'd never really noticed in scripture until fairly recently. And Hushai just blessed my socks off! But don't let my personal preference influence your choice either. Ha! Enjoy your study, sister!

Godsend No. 1 Samuel

Scripture Study: **1 Samuel 13:13–14** Samuel's "inside" knowledge about the next king of Israel. **1 Samuel 16:1–13** Samuel's first meeting with David. **1 Samuel 19:18** Samuel's meeting with David after David flees from Saul. **Psalm 99:6–7** David's description of Samuel. **Hebrews 11:32–34** What David and Samuel shared in common.

SAMUEL—A GODSEND IN DAVID'S LIFE
Under what circumstances did this Godsend become involved in David's life?
What role did this Godsend play in David's life?
What was their relationship like?
How did God use this person to influence David's life?
Have you ever had a Godsend like this in your life? If so, briefly describe this person, their role, and their impact upon your life.
Has God ever used you in a similar way to be a Godsend like this in someone else's life? If so, describe the way God used you.
At this time, is God leading you, perhaps, to become a Godsend like this in someone else's life. If so, briefly explain.
What personal insights did you gain from this study that you can apply in your own life?

GODSEND NO. 2: JONATHAN

SCRIPTURE STUDY: **1 Samuel 13:3, 14:1–15** Background on Jonathan. **1 Samuel 18:1–4**
First information on Jonathan and David's relationship; keep in mind the context and what
Jonathan had just witnessed in 1 Samuel 17. **1 Samuel 19:1–7** Information on the "triangle"
between Jonathan, Saul, and David. **1 Samuel 20** Encounter between David and Jonathan
before David flees from Saul. **1 Samuel 23:15–18** The final conversation of David and Jonathan.
2 Samuel 1:11–12, 17–27 David's response to the news of Jonathan's death.

JONATHAN—A GODSEND IN DAVID'S LIFE
Under what circumstances did this Godsend become involved in David's life?
What role did this Godsend play in David's life?
What was their relationship like?
How did God use this person to influence David's life?
Have you ever had a Godsend like this in your life? If so, briefly describe this person, their role, and their impact upon your life.
Has God ever used you in a similar way to be a Godsend like this in someone else's life? If so, describe the way God used you.
At this time, is God leading you, perhaps, to become a Godsend like this in someone else's life. If so, briefly explain.
What personal insights did you gain from this study that you can apply in your own life?

GODSEND NO. 3: NATHAN

SCRIPTURE STUDY: **2 Samuel 5:3–5** Beginning of David's reign as king. **2 Samuel 7:1–17** Nathan's influence and role in David's life. **2 Samuel 12:1–15** Nathan confronts David. (**NOTE: the previous chapter, 2 Samuel 11, is the account of David's sin with Bathsheba and his murder of her husband, Uriah.) 1 Kings 1:1–39** Nathan's role in David's last days.

NATHAN—A GODSEND IN DAVID'S LIFE
Under what circumstances did this Godsend become involved in David's life?
What role did this Godsend play in David's life?
What was their relationship like?
How did God use this person to influence David's life?
Have you ever had a Godsend like this in your life? If so, briefly describe this person, their role, and their impact upon your life.
Has God ever used you in a similar way to be a Godsend like this in someone else's life? If so, describe the way God used you.
At this time, is God leading you, perhaps, to become a Godsend like this in someone else's life. If so, briefly explain.
What personal insights did you gain from this study that you can apply in your own life?

GODSEND NO. 4: JOAB

SCRIPTURE STUDY: **2 Samuel 8:15–16** Joab's position in David's kingdom. **2 Samuel 13:37–39 and 2 Samuel 14** Joab's involvement in David and Absalom's (his son) strained relationship. (**NOTE: 2 Samuel 13 is the account of Absalom's vengeance and slaying of his brother, Amnon, who had raped their sister, Tamar.**) **2 Samuel 19:1–8** Joab confronts David as he mourns Absalom's death. (**NOTE: Though they had been reunited in 2 Samuel 14, Absalom's bitterness toward his father remained and grew, resulting in a calculated effort by Absalom to seize the kingdom from his father, David. In his effort to do this, Absalom was killed—by Joab—in battle.**) **2 Samuel 24:1–17** Joab's warning to David.

JOAB—A GODSEND IN DAVID'S LIFE
Under what circumstances did this Godsend become involved in David's life?
What role did this Godsend play in David's life?
What was their relationship like?
How did God use this person to influence David's life?
Have you ever had a Godsend like this in your life? If so, briefly describe this person, their role, and their impact upon your life.
Has God ever used you in a similar way to be a Godsend like this in someone else's life? If so, describe the way God used you.
At this time, is God leading you, perhaps, to become a Godsend like this in someone else's life. If so, briefly explain.
What personal insights did you gain from this study that you can apply in your own life?

GODSEND NO. 5 HUSHAI

SCRIPTURE STUDY: **1 Chronicles 27:33** Hushai's (and Ahithophel's) relationship to David. **2 Samuel 15:30–37** Hushai's timely appearance to David. **(NOTE: Earlier in 2 Samuel 15, David fled Jerusalem to escape from his son, Absalom, and those who conspired with Absalom to kill David.) 2 Samuel 16:15–23 and 17:1–16** Hushai's influence upon Absalom and his invaluable service to David.

HUSHAI—A GODSEND IN DAVID'S LIFE
Under what circumstances did this Godsend become involved in David's life?
What role did this Godsend play in David's life?
What was their relationship like?
How did God use this person to influence David's life?
Have you ever had a Godsend like this in your life? If so, briefly describe this person, their role, and their impact upon your life.
Has God ever used you in a similar way to be a Godsend like this in someone else's life? If so, describe the way God used you.
At this time, is God leading you, perhaps, to become a Godsend like this in someone else's life? If so, briefly explain.
What personal insights did you gain from this study that you can apply in your own life?

Day Four

1. Allow today's passage to usher you into your study of "giants." God's Word is a priceless resource bringing us comfort, reviving our strength, and renewing our courage even in the face of life's biggest giants!

> *This is my comfort in my affliction, that*
> *Thy word has revived me.* Psalm 119:50

In today's homework, you will study some of the literal and figurative giants David faced. Read the following passage, then answer the questions given.

2. 1 Samuel 17:1–33, 41–44 (You read some but not all of this in last week's lesson.)

   a. Who is the literal giant in this biblical account?

   b. According to verses 11 and 24, how were the soldiers of Israel reacting to this giant?

   c. How many days had the giant taunted the armies of Israel (verse 16)?

   d. When David first saw the giant (verse 23), how did he respond (verse 26)?

Before David ever picks up his slingshot to kill the 9-foot, 9-inch giant, he will face three figurative giants—giants of discouragement.

   e. How does David's oldest brother, Eliab, respond to David's words (verse 28)?

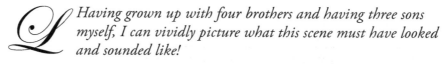

Having grown up with four brothers and having three sons myself, I can vividly picture what this scene must have looked and sounded like!

   f. David meets with Saul before he confronts Goliath. Read verses 32–33, and describe Saul's response to David's decision to fight the giant.

g. David approaches the giant in verse 40. Read verses 41–44, and describe the giant's response to David.

h. Summarize David's response to these three giants of discouragement.

3. Now, it's definitely time for a little personal application. Can you remember a recent or past experience when you were discouraged or misjudged by others because of your age, appearance, background, lack of experience or ability? Briefly describe that experience and how you responded. What did you learn from David's life about responding to giants of discouragement?

Some time ago, I was reading my Bible and I came across a passage about David that I'm sure I must have read before, but I'd never noted its significance. I wonder if you've ever seen or noticed it before. It's about another giant in another season of David's life. Read on. It's very interesting, and it will give us several principles about seasons and giants.

4. In 2 Samuel 21:15–17, we find David's final battle experience. Years earlier when he defeated Goliath, most scholars believe he was approximately sixteen to eighteen years old. But in 2 Samuel 21, David is quite old. Read the passage, and answer the following questions:

a. Who does David meet on this battlefield?

b. What does this giant intend to do?

c. How does David defeat this giant?

d. David's first battle (when he was young) was against the giant, Goliath. David's final battle (when he was old) was against another giant, Ishbi-Benob. Thus, David's days as a warrior are bookended by giants. As you think about this, what principles about the seasons of life and giants come to your mind?

e. Considering the passages you have just read from 1 Samuel 17 and 2 Samuel 21, who stood with David and delivered him in both of his encounters with giants? Explain your answer and note any principles that would apply regarding seasons and giants.

Thy word is a lamp to my feet, and a light to my path.
Psalm 119:105

The unfolding of Thy words gives light.
Psalm 119:130

Insights

5. How has the Lord spoken to you today through your study? What insights have you gleaned from His Word to apply to your own life? Take a few minutes to express your impressions in writing.

_____

_____

_____

_____

_____

_____

_____

Day Five

1. The giants we face each season often paralyze us with fear and dread. Are you facing any giants in your own life today? If so, let the truth from Psalm 119:45 encourage you to find freedom and liberty as you seek truth from your study today. Put down your pen. Before you write one word, spend a few minutes in prayer claiming today's Psalm.

And I will walk in liberty, for
I seek Thy precepts. Psalm 119:45

2. Today you will complete your study on the giants in David's life. The following passages describe some of the figurative giants David faced during the seasons of his life. Read each passage, then complete the sentence by describing in your own words the type of "giant" David encountered. To help you get started, the first sentence has been completed for you.

   a. 1 Samuel 18:9 and 29, 23:14—Sometimes a giant can be…

   someone in authority over you who wants to harm or destroy you.

   b. 1 Samuel 27:1–7 and 30:1–6—Sometimes a giant can be…

   c. 2 Samuel 11—Sometimes a giant can be…

   d. 2 Samuel 15:1–14—Sometimes a giant can be…

   e. 2 Samuel 18:31–33 (David learns of Absalom's death.)—Sometimes a giant can be…

   f. 1 Chronicles 21:1—Sometimes a giant can be…

   g. 1 Kings 1:1—Sometimes a giant can be…

Before you do your weekly reflection and journal time, I have one final passage I'd like you to study as we conclude our study on giants. If you're facing any giants today, I pray this passage will renew your courage and reignite your faith in God.

3. Read 2 Samuel 22:1–40, then answer the following questions:

    a.   According to verse 1, when did David write this Psalm?

    b.   According to verses 4a, 7a, and 21b–25, what did David do as he faced all of his giants?

    c.   According to verses 4 and 7, what should our first response be to the giants we face? When we respond like this, what can we be assured of?

    d.   According to verses 21–25, what part does our obedience play as we battle giants?

    e.   According to verses 21b–25, how could David say this was true when scripture clearly reveals his own personal sin and failures? What does this reveal about God? What does this reveal about David?

4. It is time for a few final questions for application: How do your own past sins and failures affect the battles you face today? Do they discourage and defeat you? How do they affect your relationship with God during difficult seasons as you face challenging giants?

5. Today if you have confessed and repented of your sin, will you accept God's forgiveness and unconditional love for you? If so, lift up your hands to the Lord right now and spend a moment praising Him for the clean hands and the pure heart He has so graciously given you. Then with your Bible opened to 2 Samuel 22 in one hand, and with your other hand lifted before God, read and confess the truths from verses 2–4 aloud to the Lord who hears you.

6. Finally, as you reflect upon the things you have learned and the impressions you have received this week from the Lord, journal your thoughts below.

My Journal

THIS WEEK THE LORD...

_____
_____
_____
_____
_____
_____
_____
_____
_____
_____
_____

AS A RESULT, I...

_____
_____
_____
_____
_____
_____
_____
_____
_____
_____
_____

Before you close your workbook, I feel led to give you an awesome scripture I've had on my heart as I've written this lesson. I think it will especially encourage you if you are currently facing a giant.

The prophet Jeremiah obediently delivered God's message to the dull, callous ears of Israel prior to their captivity in Babylon. His message was received with contempt and rage. As a result, Jeremiah was chained and beaten by his own people. Jeremiah 20:7–10 recounts his lament and complaint to God regarding the giants of rejection and reproach he faced from those who had even once been his friends.

In verse 11, however, we see beyond Jeremiah's tears as he expresses his deep and abiding faith in God, and this is the verse God has placed upon my heart to share with you. If you are at a place where you feel totally alone and without a Godsend, or if you are at a place where all you can see are the enormous giants threatening to destroy you, claim these words penned by Jeremiah and inspired by God, our steadfast Champion:

But the Lord is with me like a mighty warrior; so my persecutors will stumble and not prevail. Jeremiah 20:11 (NIV)

My sister, take heart and be encouraged. Your God—who is "a mighty warrior" and a steadfast Champion—is standing with you. Believe it!

In Every Season: Godsends and Giants

I. **Godsends:** the _____ and _____ people God sends into our lives to impact our lives for His divine purposes.

II. **Principles we learn from the Godsends in David's life:**

Godsend # 1—Samuel

1. They may _____ and _____ God's anointing/call upon our lives before we even become aware of it ourselves. *1 Sam. 16:10–13*

2. They are people we can _____, they're "_____." *1 Sam. 19:18*

Godsend # 2—Jonathan

3. They may be our _____, and may eventually become our dearest friend. *1 Sam. 18:1–3*

4. Our relationship with them may be _____ in _____, but the effects of the relationship will _____ us for the rest of our lives. *2 Sam. 21:7*

Godsend # 3—Nathan

5. They will be a source of sound, timely, and _____ _____ enabling us to _____ God's will for our lives. *2 Sam. 7:1–17, 1 Ki. 1:5–39*

6. They will _____ us when we sin, and will tell us the truth, the whole truth, and nothing but the truth in order to bring us to _____ and _____. *2 Sam. 12:1–15*

Godsend # 4—Hushai

7. God often sends them when we are experiencing a season of _____ / _____. *2 Sam. 15:23, 30*

8. They often show up as _____ to our _____. *2 Sam. 15:31–37*

Godsend # 5—Joab

9. They enable us to see our _____ _____. *2 Sam. 19:1–8*

10. They will not always be completely without _____, but God can still use them in our lives for His good purposes. *1 Kings 2:5–6*

III. **Giants:** the difficult circumstances, people, trials, and testings God sovereignly allows us to face in order to _____ our faith and increase our _____ upon Him.

IV. **Four Types of Giants:**

1. _____—who seeks to _____ us. *1 Pet. 5:8, Eph. 6:10–18*

   Our response:
   - Be _____ and on the alert.
   - _____ him, firm in your faith.
   - Put on the spiritual _____ of God.

2. _____—"giants" of our own making. *Jas. 1:14–15, Gal. 5:16, Rom. 6:11–14*

   Our response:
   - _____ by the Spirit.
   - Consider yourself _____ to sin and _____ to God.
   - Do not let _____ _____ in your life.
   - Present your body to God as an _____ of _____.

3. _____—an _____ ; a living, breathing person. *2 Tim. 4:14–17, Matt. 5:44, 6:14–15*

   Our response:
   - Be on _____.
   - Rely upon and _____ in God's presence and strength.
   - _____ for your enemies.
   - _____ your enemies.

4. _____—trials and testings God sovereignly allows us to experience. *Jas. 1:2–4*

   Our response:
   - _____ them as a _____ *because …*
   - They _____ our faith;
   - They produce _____;
   - They _____ / _____ us.

V. **Principles we learn from the Giants in David's life:**

1. We will face giants throughout our _____ lifetime.

2. We will never face a giant _____.
   - God is always with us, and
   - He often sends Godsends to help us.

3. We may not defeat every giant in every battle, but we can repent, be cleansed and press on with _____ _____ as David did.

The Seasons of Your Life

As I write this study, I am 45 years old—right in the big middle of mid-life. From this increasingly wrinkled vantage point, I can reflect upon many seasons that have come and gone in my life. As I do, I am deeply impressed by the uniqueness of each season. Each occurred at a unique and specific time in my life. Each had its own unique set of circumstances and challenges. Each had its own unique joys and sorrows. Each included unique people, places, and events.

More importantly, however, from this mid-life perspective, I am now able to see with greater clarity how each season of my life was uniquely used by God. But make no mistake, my hindsight is not even close to being 20/20. As I seek to fully understand the ways and purposes of God, my limited sight is confirmed by 1 Corinthians 13:12, "For now we see in a mirror dimly, but then face to face; now I know in part, but then I shall know fully just as I also have been fully known." Yes, I can see some of God's purposes and some of the ways in which He was working through the seasons of my life—but only "dimly." Even with my best pair of bifocals, I can only see glimpses of His purposes and glimmers of His insight.

In a season some years ago, God allowed a Great Storm to blow into my life. At the time, the waves from that storm engulfed me in great distress and deep sorrow. I could not even begin to see God's purposes for such a tempest nor could I fully understand His ways. Still, I clung to Him until the storm subsided.

In the aftermath of the storm, I surveyed the wreckage. Immediately I recognized my pride had been broken, my heart had been humbled, and my faith had been tested. In brokenness and desperation, I sought God for the answer to the one-word question that plagued me: Why? He answered and revealed "in part" (1 Corinthians 13:12) only what He wanted me to know at that particular point in time. He had allowed the storm to come because my pride *had* to be broken, my heart *had* to be humbled, and my faith *had* to be tested. And…He was exactly right.

But God had other purposes for the storm that were not, at first, as obvious for me to see. The ravages of the storm had taken an enormous physical, emotional, and spiritual toll on me. My wounds were deep. For months, and months, and months, God was my Healer, my Great Physician, and the Lover of my soul. In my broken, wounded condition, He tenderly, graciously, and mercifully ministered to me.

Through that process, God allowed me to see "in part" (1 Corinthians 13:12) a little more of His purpose for the storm. He wanted to teach me firsthand the truth of Lamentations 3:22–23, "The Lord's lovingkindnesses indeed never cease, for His compassions never fail. They are new every morning; great is Thy faithfulness." As a result of the storm, I experienced the fullness of His love, the endlessness of His compassion, and the greatness of His faithfulness in ways I had never before known. The storm had allowed me to know Him more intimately, and to love Him more completely.

There is a **Season**

It has been years since the Great Storm blew into my life, but those years have brought an even deeper understanding of God's purpose. In his classic devotional book, *My Utmost for His Highest*, Oswald Chambers writes:

> *If you yourself do not cut the lines that tie you to the dock, God will have to use a storm to sever them and to send you out to sea…If you believe in Jesus, you are not to spend all your time in the calm waters just inside the harbor, full of joy, but always tied to the dock. You have to get out past the harbor into the great depths of God…*[5]

It took several years for me to fully realize how true Chambers' words were and how much they applied to my own storm experience.

Several years before the storm clouds ever began to gather, God had patiently and persistently been calling me to follow Him to a new place. But I continued to cling to the calm harbor—the comfort zone of the status quo in my service to Him. God sent the storm to "send me out to sea"[6] to take me to a new place where I would discover His will for my life. And when I think about the prophet Jonah, I feel fortunate that the storm was sufficient enough to teach me! In the future, when (not if) the winds of change blow and I hear His clear call, "Follow Me," I will set sail. I will follow Him by faith. I have absolutely no desire to see or smell the "innards" of a great fish!

I've shared with you some of the things God taught me through the season of my Great Storm, but what about you? Have you examined the seasons of your life? Have you sought to discern God's purposes for each season? In the weeks ahead, we will be learning some liberating principles that will enable us to press on and to navigate successfully through the remaining seasons of our lives. But before we can focus on future seasons, we must carefully examine the current and past seasons of our lives.

This week you will be examining and evaluating the seasons of your own life. Your homework will guide you through this process. **The goal of this examination is that you will gain insight, understanding, and wisdom regarding God's purpose for each season of your life.** The Holy Spirit will faithfully guide you toward this goal. Consequently, this lesson has the potential to be used by God in an extremely significant way in your life.

At the risk of sounding incredibly negative and depressing, I must share something with you that I believe is absolutely true: those who lead unexamined lives are destined to experience a vicious cycle of repetitive, recurrent problems and a life of almost certain futility. But let me also share with you another truth that is incredibly positive and uplifting: those who allow God to direct them to examine their lives will gain understanding, insight, and wisdom which will enable them to experience a life of purpose, meaning, and eternal significance.

Sometimes, for many different reasons (busyness, weariness, guilt, shame, fear, anger, or despair), we neglect to allow God to lead us to examine our lives. We allow life's seasons to come and go without ever seeking to understand His purposes in them. As a result, our lives become shallow, a succession of seasons bereft of meaning and value. That is exactly the kind of life Solomon was experiencing when he penned the words we read in our first week of study, "Vanity of vanities! All is vanity. What advantage does man have in all his work which he does under the sun?" (Ecclesiastes 1:2–3). In Ecclesiastes, God used the vanity of Solomon's circumstances to bring him to a place where he would finally examine his life in light of God's supreme and sovereign purposes. Could that possibly be what God wants to do in this season of your life?

God has a purpose for each season. This week, will you allow God to examine your life? Will you earnestly seek to understand His purpose for each season? If you will, the wisdom you gain will allow you to grow in your walk with Him, to know Him in a more intimate way and, perhaps, to rediscover His glorious and meaningful plan for your life. Take it from someone who survived a Great Storm: Don't wait for the waves of a stormy season to force you "out to sea"[7] in your walk with God. This week, let go of the status quo. Set sail. Follow God.

Day One

1. This week's study will focus on examining the seasons of your life. Please use today's scripture to express to God in prayer your desire to examine your life by looking into the mirror of His Word.

    I considered my ways, and turned my feet to Thy testimonies. Psalm 119:59

2. Before you begin to examine the seasons of your life, there are four truths about life you need to observe and understand. These four truths are found in Ecclesiastes 3:1 and 11. Please read these two verses and complete the following:

    a. Using words directly from the text, write out the first truth about life from verse 1.

    Truth #1:

    b. In order to clarify this truth, fill in the blank in the following statement and note why the word you have added is significant.

    There is a season for _____ in life.

    c. The second truth about life is found in the first part of verse 11. Using words from the text, write out that truth.

    Truth #2:

     d.   What has God made beautiful or appropriate?

     e.   When does God make everything beautiful or appropriate?

     f.   What do you learn about God from this truth?

     g.   The third and fourth truths about life are found in the remainder of verse 11. Consider the verse carefully, and write out these truths:
Truth #3:

Truth #4:

     h.   Meditate on these two truths and explain what you believe they mean.
NOTE: If you have an Amplified Bible or any Bible study helps or commentaries, please use them to gain further insight into Ecclesiastes 3:11. If you have any computer Bible programs, please use them as well. Or go online and use Bible commentary sources (such as www.bibleclassics.com, www.biblegateway.com, and www.studylight.org) to research Ecclesiastes 3:11.

3.   One of the most well-known verses in the New Testament is Romans 8:28:

> *And we know that God causes all things to work together for good to those who love God, to those who are called according to His purpose.*

For a greater understanding of this wonderful verse and to see how it relates to the four truths you have just seen in Ecclesiastes 3, please read Romans 8:18–39 and answer the following questions:

     a.   According to verse 18, what will we experience throughout the seasons of our lives and what will we experience in the future?

b.   How does Romans 8:28 correlate with the first two truths you saw in Ecclesiastes 3:1 and 11a?

c.   According to Romans 8:31–34, what can you be assured of in every season of your life? In other words, how are God the Father and God the Son actively working on your behalf throughout the seasons of your life?

d.   According to Romans 8:35–39, even through the difficult seasons of life, what never changes? What does this passage teach you about yourself and about your relationship with God?

4.   It is time for some personal application of the passages you have studied today. Honestly answer the following questions:

a.   Do you believe and fully accept the truths from Ecclesiastes 3 and Romans 8? Why or why not?

b.   Will you willingly submit to the four truths from Ecclesiastes in regard to your own past, present, and future seasons of life? If you will, take these truths before the Lord and personalize them by praying this prayer:

> *Lord, I believe and accept that this season, every season past, and every season to come is Your season for my life (verse 1). Lord, I believe and accept that this season, every season past, and every season to come has divine purpose and is appropriate for me (verse 11a). And Lord, although I cannot fully see the eternal value and purpose of each season of my life today, I believe and accept by faith that you will reveal this to me in the future (verse 11c).*

Dear sister, I know it may be very difficult to submit to these truths from God's Word if heartache and hurt from past and present seasons continue to bring you pain and cause you to question God's purposes. But I encourage you to rest in the promises of Romans 8:35–39. Be assured of His inseparable love for you and the power He has given you to "overwhelmingly conquer" every giant in your past, present, and future.

*Thy word is a lamp
to my feet, and a
light to my path.*
Psalm 119:105

*The unfolding of Thy
words gives light.*
Psalm 119:130

5. How has the Holy Spirit spoken to you today through your study? What truths does He want you to embrace and apply to your life? Briefly record any "light" He has given you?

_____

_____

_____

_____

_____

_____

_____

_____

Day Two

1. Before you even open your Bible or pick up your pen, spend some time with the Lord in prayer. Thank Him for all He is doing in your life, and acknowledge the specific ways you see Him working in this season of your life.

*Thou hast dealt well with Thy servant,
O Lord, according to Thy word.* Psalm 119:65

IMPORTANT NOTE REGARDING THE REMAINDER OF THIS WEEK'S HOMEWORK:

For the rest of this week, your homework will involve two parts. Part I will be a study of the seasons of Joseph's life. Part II will be a personal timeline you will create to help you examine and evaluate the seasons of your life. Each day complete Part I (the study of Joseph) first, then do Part II (your timeline).

PART I: THE LIFE OF JOSEPH

2. Read Genesis 37, and answer the following questions:

   a. How old was Joseph in this chapter (verse 2)?

   b. Why did his brothers hate him (verses 3–4, 8, 11)?

   c. Where is Joseph at the conclusion of this chapter (verse 36)?

3. Read Genesis 39, and answer the following questions:

    a.   What repeated phrase or theme did you see in this chapter (verses 2–3, 21, 23)?

    b.   What injustice occurs to Joseph in this chapter (verse 20)?

    c.   At the conclusion of this chapter, where is Joseph, and what are his circumstances?

    d.   What do you learn about the seasons of life from Genesis 37 and 39?

Insights

4. What did you learn from the life of Joseph that you can apply to your own life regarding unjust circumstances, servanthood, integrity, and faith?

Thy word is a lamp to my feet, and a light to my path.
Psalm 119:105

The unfolding of Thy words gives light.
Psalm 119:130

Part II: Personal Timeline

5. Your remaining assignment today is simple. Please read the Instructions on the following pages, then study and scan pages 84–91. This assignment will help prepare you for the actual "hands on" work you will begin tomorrow.

Personal Timeline Instructions

Tomorrow you will begin constructing a timeline of the seasons of your life. You will have three days to complete your timeline.

Your timeline will be unique and will express the various seasons of your life from your birth until the present. Think of your timeline as an overview of the milestone events, experiences, seasons, and people God has most used to shape you into the person you are today. **There is no right or wrong way to complete your timeline except that it must be completed in chronological order with exact or approximate dates or descriptions noted.**

Listed below are the various components you will include on your timeline:

- *Figurative Seasons:* See pages 52–53 of your Week Three homework. Figurative seasons mirror nature's seasons. Brief descriptions of figurative seasons are listed below:

  Spring   A season of joy, peace, routine responsibilities, new beginnings, and growth.

  Summer   A season when life heats up with new opportunities, responsibilities, intense busyness, and an accelerated pace.

  Fall   A season when the winds of change blow and cause us to feel unsteady, uneasy, and unsure.

  Winter   A season of prolonged challenges and difficult circumstances when life seems cold and hard, and we feel isolated and alone.

- *Spiritual Seasons:* Salvation, spiritual growth, brokenness, renewal, etc.

- *Physiological Seasons:* See page 34 of your Week Two homework.

- *Significant Events:* Such as your wedding, pregnancies, births, moves, divorce/remarriage, deaths, etc.

- *Significant Experiences:* From your childhood, teen, and adult years.

- *Godsends:* The significant people God has used in your life; see pages 61–65 of your Week Four homework.

- *Giants:* The battles you have faced with difficult circumstances, difficult people, and your own sin; see pages 66–71 of your Week Four homework.

- *God's Purposes:* What God taught you and how He used that season in your life.

Clip and Paste Timeline Art has been created to represent each of the components listed above. Please use this artwork as you create and complete your own personal timeline. But if you are creative and you enjoy drawing, feel free to draw symbols or small pictures to represent and express these components.

On the following pages, you will find these three items:

1) Pages 84–85: A blank timeline entitled "**The Seasons of My Life**."
   You will create your own personal timeline on these pages.

2) Pages 86–87: A **Sample Timeline** of Laurie's life provided as an example
   for you as you create your own personal timeline.

3) Pages 89–91: **Clip and Paste Timeline Art** provided to help you complete
   your own personal timeline.

Please Note:

1. You have total freedom in your timeline design. Do not feel you must use all
   of the Clip and Paste Timeline Art. Use it only as needed.

2. In addition to the Clip and Paste Timeline Art, you will probably want to
   add your own special touches, symbols, or even brief word descriptions to
   your timeline.

3. If you are doing this study with a group, be assured no one will see your
   timeline unless you so desire. You will discuss your timeline with your small
   group, but you will not be expected or obligated to share everything on your
   timeline with your group members.

4. **Above all, please remember the ultimate goal of this assignment: to gain
   insight, understanding and wisdom regarding God's purpose for each
   season of your life.**

The Seasons of My Life

Your Birth

Present

*"To everything
there is a season,
and a time to every purpose
under the heaven"*

Sample Timeline

The Seasons of My Life: Laurie Cole

Your Birth

Born
1/13/58

Significant Experiences in my
Childhood Years
raised by
Christian
parents

Significant Event
Wedding
1978

Our 1st son! David

Significant Event:
Birth
7/10/81

Spiritual Season:
Salvation
1965 or so

Although I can't
remember the exact
year of my salvation,
I vividly remember
two things: 1) the
conviction of the Holy
Spirit as He made me
aware of my sin and
my need for a Savior,
and 2) the peace I
experienced when I
gave my life to Christ.

Spiritual Season:
Brokenness
1980

Through a difficult
season in my early
married life, God
broke me. This
brokenness resulted
in renewal.

Significant
Event
1982

After many years of
questioning His salvation,
my husband, Bill, became
a Christian. Hallelujah!

Spiritual Season:
Renewal
1980

I began to develop a
more intimate relationship
with the Lord than I'd
ever known before.

Our 2nd son! Kevin

Significant Event:
Birth
4/25/84

Significant Events
Moves
9/84

to Amarillo, TX
where Bill served
as min. of music
at San Jacinto Bapt.

Figurative Season:
Spring
1984-1987

Season of joyous
young motherhood
and greater spiritual
growth.

Godsends
Georgia Kern
Glenda Coffey

My Bible study leader
& my pastor's wife
who encouraged and
mentored me.

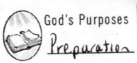
God's Purposes
Preparation

Amarillo was where
God taught me how
to study His Word
and was also where
He revealed to me
my spiritual gift
of teaching.

Significant Events
Moves
2/88

to Houston, TX
where Bill began
serving as min. of
music at Sagemont
church.

Our 3rd son! J.J.

Birth –
4/15/88

Figurative Season
Winter
1988-1990

Season of loneliness,
isolation, difficult
circumstances, and
fluctuating hormones
all of which resulted
in ↓

Battles with
Giants
Depression

God's Purposes
Spir. Growth

God used that tough
season to test and
teach me the truth
of Is. 61:3, "put on
the garment of praise
for the spirit of
heaviness," so that I
would learn how to
live above my
circumstances.

Figurative Season:
Summer
1991-1999

Busy, wild, wonderfull
years of raising sons,
keeping house, teaching
Bible studies, overseeing
homework and school
projects, running the
boys to Little League,
soccer, piano lessons,
etc!

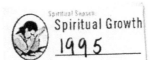
Spiritual Season:
Spiritual Growth
1995

In the midst of there
busy years, I was
becoming a burned-out,
miserable mess. This
is when God taught me
the truths of the seasons
of life and the
principles of Contentment
that transformed my
life.

Spiritual Season
Great Storm

God used this to
ultimately redirect
my life in brand
new ways.

Godsends
Janet Valentine
Scott Head

Janet invited
me to write a
Bible study for
the women of
our church.
Scott volunteered
to do the design
and layout.

Present

Significant
Experience
2003

God enabled
me to write
There is a
Season.

*"To everything
there is a season,
and a time to every purpose
under the heaven"*

The Seasons of Your Life

CLIP AND PASTE TIMELINE ART

This artwork has been designed for you to use as you create your personal timeline. Remove these pages from your workbook if it will make it easier for you to clip and organize your work. Use tape or a glue stick to affix the artwork to your timeline. Use the blank provided on each design to record dates or brief descriptions.

The Seasons of Your Life

CLIP AND PASTE TIMELINE ART

This artwork has been designed for you to use as you create your personal timeline. Remove these pages from your workbook if it will make it easier for you to clip and organize your work. Use tape or a glue stick to affix the artwork to your timeline. Use the blank provided on each design to record dates or brief descriptions.

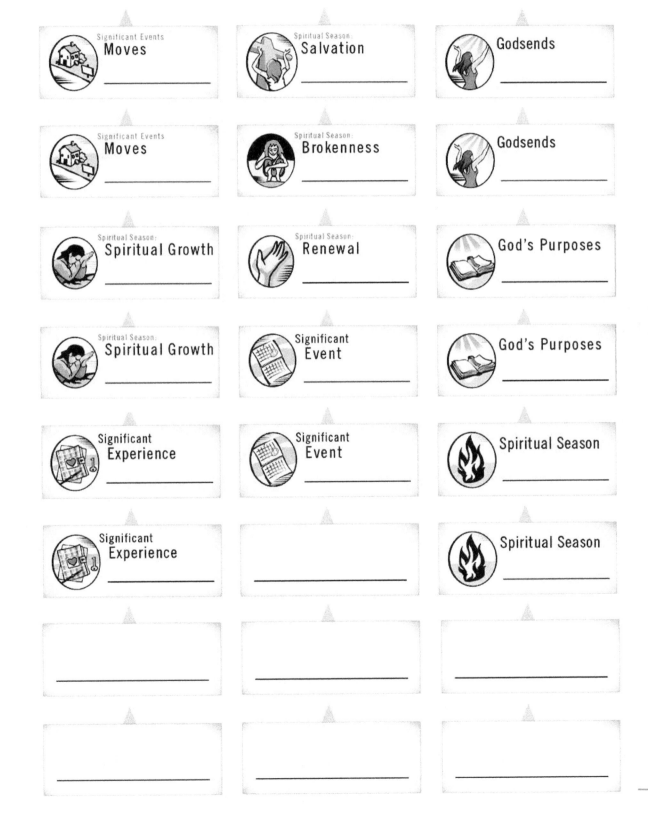

The Seasons of Your Life

Day Three

1. Prayerfully begin your time in God's Word today using the scripture from Psalm 119.

> *Teach me good discernment and knowledge, for*
> *I believe in Thy commandments.* Psalm 119:66

PART I: THE LIFE OF JOSEPH

2. Today you will continue your overview and study of the life of Joseph. Please read Genesis 40, then answer the following questions:

   a. According to verse 8, who does Joseph credit with his ability to interpret dreams, and what does this reveal about Joseph's character?

   b. According to verse 23, what additional setback did Joseph experience in this season of his life?

3. Please read Genesis 41, then answer the following questions:

   a. According to verse 1, how many years have passed since Joseph had interpreted the cupbearer's dream?

   b. As Joseph stands before Pharoah, who does Joseph again credit with his ability to interpret dreams? According to verse 39, did Pharoah recognize the source of Joseph's ability to interpret dreams?

   c. Briefly describe Joseph's position and duties in Egypt according to verses 40–45.

   d. How old was Joseph when he stood before Pharoah (verse 46)? Scan verses 47–57 to calculate how old Joseph was at the conclusion of this chapter. How old was he?

e. Joseph was seventeen years old when he was sold by his brothers into slavery and taken from Canaan to Egypt. He was thirty years old when he interpreted Pharoah's dream. Quickly calculate and write out the number of years Joseph was unjustly imprisoned: _____ years. Circle the season that would best describe this time period in Joseph's life:

winter   *spring*   *summer*   *fall*

What truth does this reveal about the potential length of a season of life?

f. In Genesis 41:49, seven additional years have passed as Joseph has served Pharoah and the people of Egypt. Joseph is now thirty-seven years old. Quickly review your answer to question "c" above regarding Joseph's position and duties in his service to Pharoah. Circle the season that would best describe this seven-year time period in Joseph's life:

winter   *spring*   *summer*   *fall*

g. In Genesis 41:50–52, you learned Joseph became the father of two sons prior to this famine. He is thirty-seven years old and he has been in service to Pharoah for seven years. According to the names Joseph gave his sons, what has God done in this seven-year season of Joseph's life? What does this reveal about God? What does this reveal about the seasons of life?

h. One final mathematical question regarding Joseph: using the information you now have from previous questions above, how many total years has Joseph been in Egypt? _____ years

Thy word is a lamp to my feet, and a light to my path.
Psalm 119:105

The unfolding of Thy words gives light.
Psalm 119:130

Insights

4. As you have studied the life of Joseph, what insights has the Holy Spirit revealed to you about the seasons of your life, your faith, and your relationship with God?

_____

_____

_____

_____

_____

_____

_____

There is a Season

PART II: PERSONAL TIMELINE

5. Begin creating your personal timeline using the instructions given on pages 82–83.

6. Pace yourself on this assignment. Remember, you will have two more days to complete your timeline.

Day Four

1. Spend a few minutes with the Lord in prayer before you delve into your Bible study. Pray through the following Psalm praising Him for His goodness to you, seeking His divine instructions as you observe and study His Word.

Thou art good and doest good;
teach me Thy statutes. Psalm 119:68

PART I: THE LIFE OF JOSEPH

2. Read Genesis 42, then answer the following questions:

    a. Twenty-plus years have passed since Joseph's brothers have seen him. When they arrive in Egypt, they don't recognize Joseph—although he recognizes them. According to verse 5, what brought them to Egypt?

    b. From Joseph's perspective, what had brought his brothers to Egypt (verses 6 and 9)?

    c. In verse 11, Joseph's brothers describe themselves to Joseph. Is their description and perspective about themselves true? Explain your answer.

    d. Joseph disguises himself from his brothers, and appears harsh to them throughout the entire chapter. Why may Joseph have behaved in this way to his brothers? Was he bitter? Was he getting even? Explain your answer.

e. According to verses 21–22, and 28, what did Joseph's brothers realize in their desperate situation? What was God doing in this season of their lives?

f. What did you learn about Joseph's true feelings toward his brothers from verses 23–24? Why did he weep?

3. Read Genesis 43, and answer the following questions:

a. Why is the scene in Genesis 43:26 significant (review Genesis 37:7 if necessary)?

b. One final move in this chapter by Joseph produces shock and causes his brothers to again recognize something very significant is happening to them. What happened at dinner? What do you think they may have discussed among themselves while Joseph sat at another table—and listened?

Thy word is a lamp to my feet, and a light to my path.
Psalm 119:105

The unfolding of Thy words gives light.
Psalm 119:130

Insights

4. As you have studied Joseph's life today, what insights has the Lord given you to apply to your own life and to your relationships with others? How is God speaking to you?

_____

_____

_____

_____

_____

_____

_____

PART II: PERSONAL TIMELINE

5. Continue working on your personal timeline.

6. Ask the Lord to speak to you and give you brand new insights into the seasons of your life. Perhaps your study of Joseph has also given you additional insights as to God's purposes in your life.

I realize you have worked long and hard this week on your lesson, and I'm so thankful for your diligence. Right now I so want to encourage you as you continue creating your timeline. I just cannot stress enough the benefits you will receive from completing it. In fact, it may very well be the most important assignment of this entire study for you. As I have written this study, God has led me to be very transparent with you about the seasons of my own life. In this timeline assignment, I'm asking you to be very transparent, too. As the Lord brings things to light and gives you His viewpoint and perspective regarding the seasons of your life, be open and honest. And keep in mind John 8:32, "and you shall know the truth, and the truth shall make you free." Truth liberates. My dear sister, let His truth set you free!

Day Five

1. Begin your final day of study in prayer. The Psalm you will use in your prayer time is so beautiful in light of our study this week. The question is, can you pray this verse to God and mean it with all of your heart? If you can, please do. If you cannot, be honest with the Lord and tell Him you're just not able to yet. Then ask Him to so work in your heart that one day, very soon, you *will* be able to see His good purposes in your affliction.

> *It is good for me that I was afflicted, that*
> *I may learn Thy statutes.* Psalm 119:71

PART I: THE LIFE OF JOSEPH

2. Today, the story of Joseph comes to a climax. Begin your study by reading Genesis 44 and 45, then answer the following questions:

   a. Joseph tests his brothers one final time in Genesis 44. As a result, what do the brothers think will happen to Benjamin? According to Genesis 44:13–16, how do they respond? What do they fully admit?

b. Read Genesis 42:24, 43:30–31, 45:1–2 and note the progression of Joseph's emotions. What do you think may have made Joseph finally lose control and weep before his brothers? What may God have been doing in Joseph's heart from the time he first saw his brothers in Genesis 42?

c. According to Genesis 45:5–8, what does Joseph now know about God's purposes in allowing him to be sold by his brothers into slavery and taken to Egypt? When do you think he began to understand this?

Repentance, forgiveness, and restoration have come about between Joseph and his brothers. Joseph's entire family then moves to Egypt where Joseph, with Pharoah's complete approval, provides for his family's every need for the rest of their lives. You might think that the preservation of Joseph's family would be purpose enough for God to allow Joseph to endure and experience all that he did during those twenty-plus years he was in Egypt. But God's purposes exceeded that. God had a much bigger picture in mind when He sovereignly allowed Joseph to suffer and to succeed.

3. Read Genesis 12:1–2a and 47:27 and Exodus 1:6–7, then record God's greater purpose for Joseph's suffering and success.

4. One final question about Joseph: how is Joseph like Christ?

PART II: PERSONAL TIMELINE

5. Finish your timeline noting any new insights you may have received from the Lord.

6. If you have time, please use your journal page to sum up what the Lord has done in your life this week.

My Journal

THIS WEEK THE LORD...

_____
_____
_____
_____
_____
_____
_____
_____

AS A RESULT, I...

_____
_____
_____
_____
_____
_____
_____
_____

After I completed writing this week's lesson, one brief, haunting question consumed my thoughts: What if?

What if Joseph's brothers had never sold him into slavery?

What if Potiphar's wife had never falsely accused him?

What if he had never been imprisoned and interpreted the chief cupbearer's dream?

What if Joseph had never stood before Pharoah and interpreted his dream?

But in my mind, the greatest "what if" of all was this:

What if Joseph had not steadfastly held on to his faith and obedience to God?

God is sovereign in all of His ways. He allowed Joseph's brothers to carry out their wicked scheme setting off a chain reaction which would ultimately result in…*good—the salvation of an entire nation.*

There is, however, an equally important truth that always parallels the sovereignty of God: man has been given a free will. We have the power to choose how we will respond to the seasons of unjust suffering, sorrow, and loss that God sovereignly allows to touch our lives. Joseph chose to resist bitterness, hatred, unforgiveness, passion, lust, and pride which would ultimately reflect the God he loved and the Son He would send.

What if you, too, would accept everything God has sovereignly allowed to touch your life, and believe He even has a good purpose in all of it? What if you, too, would choose to steadfastly hold on to your faith and respond in obedience and Christlikeness in every season of your life? *What…if?*

The Seasons of Your Life

I.   **Journey Update**

   A.   **Our Destination:** _____—to be satisfied with your _____, _____, and _____ .

   B.   **Our Itinerary:** Two-Part Journey

      1.   Part I: _____ and _____ the seasons of life in order to discover your own current season of life, and to gain insight about God's purposes throughout the seasons of your life.

         Primary Process: _____

      2.   Part II: learning the _____ of _____ in order to apply them to your life in every season of your life.

         Primary Process: _____

   C.   **Final Result:** _____

II. **Today's Topic: The Struggle to Transition from Part I to Part II**

   A.   Between Part I and Part II we may still struggle with:

      1.   Many _____ _____: Why God?

      2.   Ongoing _____ and _____ from past and present circumstances.

      3.   Ongoing _____, _____, and _____.

   B.   The keys to overcoming the struggle:

      1.   _____. *Psalm 46:10*

      2.   _____ to God's sovereignty.

III. **Facts We Must Face…as learned from the life of Joseph:**

   A. God has a _____ for our lives, but Satan will attempt to _____ it. *1 Pet. 2:5–9*

   B. _____ is part of God's plan for our lives. *Phil 1:29*

   C. Others may _____ and _____ us, but God never will. *Is. 49:14–16*

   D. _____ brings bondage, but _____ brings freedom. *Gen. 45:4–8, 50:19–20*

   E. What others intend for _____, God can use for _____. *Is. 53:5, 7, 10–12*

   Joseph's response to the struggles he faced: _____

IV. **Truths We Must Embrace…to "cease striving" and submit to God's sovereignty**

   A. There is a _____ for _____ in life. *Ecc. 3:1*

   Apply: This season is _____ for my life.

   B. God has made everything beautiful/with _____ in its time. *Ecc. 3:11a*

   Apply: This season in my life has _____.

   C. God has made us long for eternal _____ in our lives. *Ecc. 3:11b*

   Apply: There is eternal _____ in this season of my life.

   D. We cannot fully _____ the eternal _____ of our lives this side of eternity. *Ecc. 3:11c*

   Apply: I may not _____ the eternal value of this season now, but _____, I believe God will _____ it in the future.

   Final Truth: The road to contentment begins with a _____.

There is a Season Part II

Experiencing Contentment in Every Season

Rejoicing in Every Season

Only a few weeks ago, I stood in a church singing along with a great congregation of my brothers and sisters in Christ. As the music minister led us, we sang the great songs of the faith:

Would you be free from the burden of sin?
There's pow'r in the blood, pow'r in the blood.
Would you o'er evil a victory win?
There's wonderful power in the blood.[8]

Come, we that love the Lord, and let our joys be known;
Join in a song with sweet accord, join in a song with sweet accord,
And thus surround the throne, and thus surround the throne.

We're marching to Zion, beautiful, beautiful Zion;
We're marching upward to Zion, the beautiful city of God.

Then let our songs abound, and every tear be dry;
We're marching thro' Immanuel's ground,
we're marching thro' Immanuel's ground,
To fairer worlds on high, to fairer worlds on high.[9]

Never in my life have I heard such powerful and glorious congregational music. At one point, I stopped singing in order to hear and experience more clearly the paean of praise from the lips of those all around me. I cannot describe in mere words the power that fell and filled that church that day, but the preacher who spoke following the music probably described it best when he said, "As we were singing, I felt as if we were as close to heaven as we could ever possibly be here on this earth."

But now I must share with you what set that glorious music, those powerful words, and that wonderful singing apart, and why I believe the presence and power of the Holy Spirit in our midst was magnified so enormously: Those songs were sung *at a funeral*.

Although no funeral is ever without pain and heartache, that particular funeral was especially difficult. Death, it seemed, had arrived far too early for the young husband and father whose funeral we now attended. Death, it also seemed, had arrived without regard to four small children who were now left without a daddy. But it was exactly those circumstances that made what I witnessed that day all the more meaningful. For in that service, I watched a grief-stricken father, a heartbroken mother, and a much-too-young widow *sing*.

Before the music began for the funeral that day, the music minister (my own, precious father) said, "As Christians, we are the only ones who can sing in the face of circumstances like these. So today, we are going to sing some of Lane's (the deceased) favorite songs about the wonderful power of the blood of Christ." So we stood, and we sang because we believe in the One who has given us a song. And as Lane's family stood and sang—even through their tears—they were a visible testimony of the *"pow'r, pow'r, wonder-working pow'r (of) the precious blood of the Lamb."*[10]

It is natural and it is even easy to sing, to praise, and to rejoice in the Lord during the sunny, blue-sky seasons of life. But it is supernatural and it is miraculous to sing and rejoice during the cold, dark seasons of the night. The psalmist writes in Psalm 42:8, "The Lord will command His lovingkindness in the daytime; and His song will be with me in the night." God has given us a song—a reason to rejoice—every day, every night, in every season of our lives.

The focus of your lesson this week will be on the supernatural, miraculous power we, as Christians, have to "rejoice evermore" (1 Thessalonians 5:16, KJV). As you study these principles of rejoicing, I pray the song He's given you will be renewed and reignited so that in every season of your life, all who witness your life will see the visible evidence of His song and will give praise and glory to the Song Giver, our magnificent and loving heavenly Father.

The Lord is my strength and song, and He has become my
salvation; this is my God, and I will praise Him… Exodus 15:2

Day One

1. As we focus on rejoicing this week, the Psalms for our prayer time each day will reflect that theme, too. Praise Him in a prayer of thanksgiving for all of His blessings—and especially for the blessing of His Word that you are about to open and for the teaching He Himself is about to give you.

Let my lips utter praise, for Thou dost
teach me Thy statutes. Psalm 119:171

This week's lesson marks a turning point in our study. In Part I, we learned to identify the seasons of life and to understand them from God's perspective. In the second part of this study, we will build upon the principles we have previously learned by adding some very valuable, practical truths that—should you choose to apply them to your life—will enable you to experience joy, meaning, and contentment in every remaining season of your life. For today only, you will briefly review some of the principles you learned in previous weeks in order to prepare you for the truths that lie ahead in your study.

NOTE: Please do not read the notes at the conclusion of today's homework until you have completed your study for today.

2. Begin your study by returning to Ecclesiastes for a review. Please read Ecclesiastes 1:1–3:8. As you read, use a pen or pencil to underline the following key words and phrases on the pages of your Bible:

- vanity/futility/meaningless
- under the sun/under heaven
- striving after the wind/chasing after the wind/vexation of spirit/grasping for the wind

3. Briefly summarize below the theme of Ecclesiastes 1:1–11.

4. Briefly summarize what Solomon determined to do and the conclusions he reached in Ecclesiastes 1:12–15.

5. How does Ecclesiastes 1:16–2:11 relate to the preceding verses in Ecclesiastes 1:13–15?

6. According to Ecclesiastes 2:15–20, how did Solomon feel after he had completed his pursuit for meaning in life?

7. Anytime you see repeated words and phrases as you study scripture, it is significant. Repetition gives you insight into the author's primary message and purpose for writing. Think about the repeated phrases you underlined in Ecclesiastes 1:1–3:8. What primary message is revealed through the repeated phrases in these verses?

8. Read the following verses and note the repeated word used in each of them.

   a. Ecclesiastes 1:8b   c. Ecclesiastes 5:10

   b. Ecclesiastes 4:8   d. Ecclesiastes 6:3, 7

   What repeated word did you see in these verses? _____

   Briefly summarize the theme and message that tie each of these verses together.

9. In order to gain a deeper understanding of the message and meaning of the book, please read through the following definitions:

   a. *Vanity/futility/meaninglessness:*[11] emptiness; fig. something transitory and unsatisfactory.

   b. *Satisfied:*[12] to sate, i.e. fill to satisfaction (lit. or fig.); have enough, satisfy.

   c. *Content:*[13] satisfied; happy.

   As you can see, the word "vanity" is the antonym (opposite) of the words "satisfied" and "content." You can also see that the words "satisfied" and "content" are synonyms (the same). **Solomon's search for meaning in life, then, is ultimately a search for contentment.**

10. In Ecclesiastes 3:1 and 11, Solomon gives us the following four truths he has come to understand through his quest for satisfaction and meaning to life:

    a. There is a season for everything in life. (Ecclesiastes 3:1–8)

    b. God has made everything beautiful, appropriate, and with purpose in its time. (Ecclesiastes 3:11a)

    c. God has made us long for eternal significance and meaning in our lives. (Ecclesiastes 3:11b)

    d. We cannot yet fully know the eternal significance, value, and purpose of our lives. (Ecclesiastes 3:11c)

11. After Solomon states the four truths of Ecclesiastes 3:1 and 11, he then reveals how to live in light of these truths. Please read Ecclesiastes 3:12–14, then list below the instructions Solomon gives.

For weeks I've been waiting to give you a couple of wonderful quotes. I did not give them to you earlier because I wanted you to arrive at your own conclusions regarding Ecclesiastes as the Spirit revealed them to you. But since you have diligently done your own study, I can finally share these great quotes with you:

> "The theme of the Book of Ecclesiastes is that 'under the sun' (i.e., without God in the picture), all is vanity."[14]
> **Spiros Zodhiates**

> "Ecclesiastes is an inspired confession of failure and pessimism when God is excluded, when man lives under the sun, and forgets the larger part, which is always over the sun, the eternal and abiding things."[15]
> **G. Campbell Morgan**

I wholeheartedly agree with the conclusions of these scholars. I would also add that I believe Ecclesiastes is the account of Solomon's search for satisfaction and contentment in life and his discovery that true satisfaction and contentment are only achieved by resting in God's sovereignty in every season of life, rejoicing, doing good, seeing good, and, above all, by fearing God.

*I have experienced firsthand the same frustrations with futility that Solomon expressed in Ecclesiastes—but on an entirely different level. As one who has primarily been a wife, mother, and homemaker, things like laundry, mopping, cleaning bathrooms, meal planning, grocery shopping, and cooking (not to mention refereeing quarrels between the feuding triangle of my own three sons) have consumed many seasons of my life. And when those tasks are completed and checked off my "To Do" list, within hours those same clothes need to be washed again, that same floor needs to be mopped again, those same bathrooms <u>definitely</u> need to be cleaned again, more meals need to be planned, more groceries need to be shopped for, and more meals need to be cooked (and, of course, one more war has broken out among the brothers which must be refereed)! When I have focused **solely** upon the vicious, seemingly futile cycle of my labor—upon **only** what I could see "under the sun" in my own little world—I have felt just like Solomon: "Vanity of vanities! All is vanity." (Ecclesiastes 1:2)*

*Dear sister, God has patiently taught me and constantly reminds me that the life He has given me is not supposed to be a vicious cycle of futility and dissatisfaction. The life He has given me is not to be lived with an earthbound focus. He has redeemed me and given me a life of joy, purpose, meaning and satisfaction despite my season or my circumstances. But I **cannot** experience this joyous, meaningful, satisfying life if I continue to focus on anything other than Him—and neither can you!*

Tomorrow we will begin to look at the principles of contentment. But for today, let me ask you several questions:

- *What season of life are you currently experiencing?*
- *Are you struggling in your life and labor in this season?*
- *Are you currently fighting despair and dissatisfaction in any area of your life?*
- *What is the primary focus of your life?*

If you, as a Christian, are not currently experiencing a life of satisfaction and contentment, let me encourage you to do something right now. Look up. Begin to focus on the One who is far over and above the sun. Tell the Lord you are weary of futility and discontentment. Ask Him to restore the joy, meaning, and abundance He has so freely given you through the precious blood of His son.

If you have never experienced the joy of salvation and the forgiveness of your sins, I want to encourage you to do the same thing: Look up. Tell the Lord you are weary of the futility of striving to earn His approval on your own merits and of striving to find satisfaction through your own efforts. Acknowledge your sin and your need for Him. Ask Him to redeem you through the precious blood of Christ. Accept by faith His gift of salvation.

Finally, if you accepted Christ as your Savior today, your next step is to make a public profession of your faith. If you are doing this study with a group, tell them about your decision to follow Christ. They will rejoice with you and will encourage you in your walk with Him. If you're doing this study on your own, find a Christ-centered, Bible-believing church in your area. Let them know about your decision, and ask them to guide you to classes their church provides to encourage and to scripturally train new believers in the faith. One more thing: welcome to the family of God, sister!

Thy word is a lamp to my feet, and a light to my path.
Psalm 119:105

The unfolding of Thy words gives light.
Psalm 119:130

Insights

12. Conclude your study by noting any "light" the Holy Spirit has given you as you studied God's Word today.

_____

_____

_____

_____

_____

_____

_____

_____

Day Two

1. Before you begin to study, take time to pray. Ask the Lord to enrich your life today through the treasure of His Word. Rejoice in the specific ways He has used His Word in your life over the past few weeks.

I rejoice in Your word, like one who finds a great treasure. Psalm 119:162 (NLT)

Good news! From this point on, the focus of our study will be on how to live a joyous, purpose-filled, satisfying life—even though we still certainly live "under the sun" here on planet Earth. Solomon's instructions to us in Ecclesiastes 3:12–14 will serve as the springboard to launch us into this second part of our study. This lesson and the ones that follow are the "really good news" lessons I mentioned in the introduction to Week Four. So, get ready, girl—we're heading toward the "Promised Land" of contentment as we learn how to become God's women in every season of our lives!

2. Today you will begin to study the topic of "joy" and "rejoicing." Even Solomon, who described life as "meaningless," saw value in joy and in rejoicing. Read Ecclesiastes 3:12a, and record what Solomon wrote.

3. Continue to study joy and rejoicing by compiling a "Reasons to Rejoice" list. Please read each scripture reference, then add your insights regarding when and why we are to rejoice on the lines provided.

REASONS TO REJOICE

❑   Matthew 5:11–12

_____

_____

❑   Luke 10:20

_____

_____

❑   Acts 5:41

_____

_____

❑   Romans 12:12, 15

_____

_____

❑   Philippians 4:4

_____

_____

❑   James 1:2–4

_____

_____

❑   1 Peter 1:3–6, 8

_____

_____

❑   1 Peter 4:13

_____

_____

_____

4. In Luke 10, Jesus sent seventy of His disciples out to spread His message of the good news of His coming and to heal the sick. They obeyed and returned to Him with news of their success. Read Luke 10:17–22, then answer the following questions:

     a.   Briefly describe the prevailing atmosphere as the disciples returned from their mission. What was the focus of their joy?

b. How did Jesus respond to this? What priority or principle was He teaching them about rejoicing?

c. Verse 21 reveals the source of Jesus' joy. What was His source of joy?

d. Please read John 15:11 and 16:22. What is the source of our joy, and how secure is it?

e. Please read Galatians 5:22. According to Galatians and to the verses you just read from John 15 and 16, what does joy reflect and give evidence of through our lives?

5. Please review your "Reasons to Rejoice" list and the scriptures you just read from Luke, John, and Galatians. How is the joy of a Christian unlike the joy of a non-Christian? Please explain your answer.

6. It is time to apply some of the truths you have studied today. Use your "Reasons to Rejoice" list to examine your own life. Prayerfully review your list once again to determine whether you are consistently and obediently rejoicing in the ways in which these scriptures teach. Place a checkmark in the box beside the scriptures you are faithfully obeying.

    If there were any boxes you could not honestly check, please read one final verse for the day: Hebrews 12:1–2.

    Right where you are, bow your head and confess to God your sin, neglect, and unwillingness to rejoice in the specific areas He's made you aware of today. Commit to: (1) "lay aside every encumbrance, and the sin which so easily entangles (you)"; (2) "run with endurance the race set before (you)"; and (3) "(fix your) eyes on Jesus." Ask God to restore your joy and give you the same eternal focus Christ had in your own seasons of suffering and pain.

7. Briefly write out any insights the Holy Spirit has shown you through His word and by His Spirit today.

_____

_____

_____

_____

_____

_____

_____

Thy word is a lamp to my feet, and a light to my path.
Psalm 119:105

The unfolding of Thy words gives light.
Psalm 119:130

Day Three

1. As always, begin your time of study in prayer. May the Psalm for today reflect the desire of your heart.

   Let my tongue sing of Thy word, for all Thy commandments are righteousness. Psalm 119:172

Today you will continue to study the topic of joy and rejoicing. Praise and singing are two ways of rejoicing and expressing our joy, and that will be the focus of our study today.

2. The first song ever recorded in scripture is found in Exodus 15. Quickly scan Exodus 14 to discover the circumstances that led to that first song.

   a. Briefly describe the circumstances that preceded the song.

   b. What motivated the Israelites to sing? In other words, why did they sing?

   c. Quickly scan Exodus 15 and describe the theme and focus of their song.

d. As Christians, how can we apply this to our own lives? What should motivate us to sing? What should the theme and focus of our singing be?

3. Through his writings, the Apostle Paul taught us a great deal about joy and rejoicing, and about praise and singing. Read the following scriptures penned by Paul and briefly note what he taught about joy, rejoicing, praise, and singing.

a. Romans 15:13—What does joy also produce?

b. Ephesians 5:18–20—When we are filled with the Spirit, how will our conversation with others and our thought life be affected?

4. Paul not only preached about praise and rejoicing, he practiced it. Please read Acts 16:16–34, then answer the following questions:

a. Why were Paul and Silas jailed?

b. How did Paul and Silas respond to their circumstances?

c. Several things happen as a result of the prayers and praise of Paul and Silas (verse 25b–33). List the results you observed.

d. At the conclusion of this account, the jailer has been saved—transformed. According to verse 34b, what has salvation produced in his life?

5. What about Jesus? Did He sing? Read the following verses, and note what you learn about our singing Savior.

   a. Hebrews 2:12—This verse quotes the Messianic prophecy from Psalm 22 which Christ fulfilled. Note what this verse teaches concerning Christ's mission and how He describes the way He fulfilled His mission. In a sense, what was Christ doing throughout His early ministry?

   b. Matthew 26:30—Note the immediate and preceding verses for a deeper understanding of the significance of this verse.

Insights   6. How has the Lord spoken to you today through your study? How has God's Word affected your life today? Record your insights.

Thy word is a lamp to my feet, and a light to my path.
Psalm 119:105

The unfolding of Thy words gives light.
Psalm 119:130

_____

_____

_____

_____

_____

_____

_____

_____

Day Four

1. In our Psalm today, David reveals the reason he longs to live and the source that sustains his life. Make the words of this Psalm your own as you spend time in prayer before beginning your study.

> *Let me live that I may praise You, and may Your laws sustain me.* Psalm 119:–175 (NIV)

Yesterday you looked at Paul's teachings on joy and rejoicing, praise, and singing. You also studied the account in Acts 16 where Paul revealed he practiced what he preached. For the next two days, you will be observing and studying Paul's example through his letter to the Philippians.

2. Today please read Philippians 1–2. As you read, please do the following:

a. Circle or underline every mention of the words "joy," "rejoice," and any synonyms.

b. In the space provided on the following pages, make notes regarding:

- what you learn about joy and rejoicing
- what you learn about Paul and his circumstances
- what you learn about Paul's attitude and example
- Paul's instructions and commands to the Philippians
- the promises Paul gives to them

As you make your notes, please be sure to include the scripture reference to which they refer.

Please *take your time*, and do not rush through this assignment.

JOY AND REJOICING

PAUL'S CIRCUMSTANCES

PAUL'S ATTITUDE AND EXAMPLE

INSTRUCTIONS AND COMMANDS

PROMISES

*Thy word is a lamp
to my feet, and a
light to my path.*
Psalm 119:105

*The unfolding of Thy
words gives light.*
Psalm 119:130

3. What has the Lord taught you through your study of Philippians? How has He spoken to you through the life of Paul? Please take time to note your insights.

_____

_____

_____

_____

_____

_____

_____

_____

Day Five

1. Please spend some time in prayer before you begin your final day of study. Praise the Lord and thank Him for the joy He has given you.

   *I have inherited Thy testimonies forever, for
   they are the joy of my heart.* Psalm 119:111

2. Conclude your study and observations of Philippians by reading chapters 3–4. As you read, remember to underline or circle every mention of the words "joy," "rejoice," and their synonyms.

3. Continue to make notes on the same topics you were given in yesterday's instructions.

JOY AND REJOICING

PAUL'S CIRCUMSTANCES

PAUL'S ATTITUDE AND EXAMPLE

INSTRUCTIONS AND COMMANDS

PROMISES

4. Please spend some time journaling and expressing what the Lord has done in your life this week and how you have chosen to respond to Him.

My *Journal*

THIS WEEK THE LORD...

_____

_____

_____

_____

_____

_____

_____

_____

AS A RESULT, I...

_____

_____

_____

_____

_____

_____

_____

_____

As we conclude this week of study, I have a confession to make. Although I am a lifelong Baptist and very conservative in my beliefs and theology, I am also—a "Kitchen Charismatic." Allow me to explain.

Years ago, I learned a key to my own survival that enables me to live above my own melancholy temperament. That key is rejoicing, praising God, singing, and worshipping Him—especially during the difficult seasons of life when I am most tempted to despair and most prone to depression.

There is a wonderful scripture that contains a "prescription," a "cure" for those times when we're discouraged and disheartened. Isaiah 61:3 says Christ has given us "the garment of praise for the spirit of heaviness" (KJV). When we are heavy in spirit, hurting, or overwhelmed in any way, this scripture encourages us to put on "the garment of praise."

I became a "Kitchen Charismatic" approximately twenty years go. At that time, God was allowing me to experience a season of testing—and I was failing that test! That's when He reminded me of Isaiah 61:3. He brought that verse to my mind one day, and He impressed me to put a cassette player in my kitchen and to begin consistently listening to praise and worship music.

During that season of my life, I used to spend hours and hours each day in the kitchen cooking and cleaning and feeding my small children. As I began listening to the beautiful praise music each day, I noticed something supernatural was beginning to happen to me: my spirit was lifting, my joy was returning, my hope was renewing, and my *focus* was changing. Soon I began memorizing those songs… and singing along…and *lifting* my hands…and rejoicing with abandon! And that's when I became…a "Kitchen Charismatic!"

That's also when I began to learn how to "pass the test" I was experiencing. God used that time of testing to teach me to praise Him in spite of my circumstances and to focus on Him and not on my circumstances. God then supernaturally enabled me to live victoriously above my circumstances. Long before God ever changed my circumstances, God changed *me*.

These days, I'm not in the kitchen as much as I used to be. I seem to be spending more time in my car—which brings me to my final point. Yes, you can be a "Kitchen Charismatic" in your car, but please remember: keep at least one hand on the steering wheel at all times! Sister, ***rejoice!***

Rejoicing in Every Season

I.   Solomon's Conclusions—*Ecc. 3:1–11*

    A.   There is a season for everything in life. *Ecc. 3:1–8*

    B.   God has made everything beautiful, appropriate, and with purpose in its time. *Ecc. 3:11a*

    C.   God has made us long for eternal significance and meaning in our lives.. *Ecc. 3:11b*

    D.   We cannot yet fully know the eternal significance, value, and purpose of our lives. *Ecc. 3:11c*

II. Solomon's Instructions—*Ecc. 3:12–14*

    A.   In this study, we will call the first three instructions the _____.

    B.   The first instruction, _____ , is the first, _____.

        1.   OT/Hebrew definition of rejoice[16]

            •   to _____ up

            •   to _____ up

            •   to be or _____ _____

        2.   Ecclesiastes teaches we are to _____…

            •   in our everyday, routine _____, and work. *Ecc. 3:22*

            •   in our labor that we consider to be _____ and unsatisfying. *Ecc. 5:19*

            •   _____ our lives; in every _____. *Ecc. 11:8–9*

III. Scripture Teaches that Joy/Rejoicing…

    A.   Is the result of _____—a work of _____. *John 16:20*

    B.   Cannot be _____ _____ from us. *John 16:22*

    C.   Is a _____, thus, a _____. *1 Thess. 5:16*

    D.   Is to be _____ _____. *1 Thess. 5:16, Phil. 4:4*

    E.   Is the opposite of _____ / _____. *Ecc. 15:24, 16–17, Numbers 14 reveals it can cost us God's blessing.*

    F.   Is often expressed in _____ and in _____. *Luke 10:21, Eph. 5:18–20.*

IV.   **Paul's Example: I can rejoice in the Lord always because…**

    A.   Christ is my _____. *Phil. 1:12–21*

        1.   Despite my _____ in life (_____). *Phil. 1:7, 13–14, 17*

        2.   By focusing on the _____ not the _____. *Phil. 1:22–23*

    B.   Christ is my _____. *Phil. 2:5–8, 17*

        1.   Despite my _____. *Phil. 2:3–4*

        2.   By focusing on _____, _____, and _____.
            Phil. 2:3–9

    C.   Christ is my _____. *Phil. 3:8–15*

        1.   Despite my _____—the _____ and the _____. *Phil. 3:4–7*

        2.   By focusing on _____ Him. *Phil. 3:8–15*

    D.   Christ is my _____. *Phil. 4:13*

        1.   Despite my _____ and _____. *Phil. 4:11–19*

        2.   By focusing on _____ and His _____. *Phil. 4:6–19*

Doing Good in Every Season

As I heard the story break on the national news, I was stunned. In shock and disbelief I thought, "This cannot possibly be true. Surely someone has reported this story all wrong," I waited anxiously for a rebuttal—but none came. Instead, there was further confirmation. The story, indeed, was true. My heart sank. One of our country's premier spokesmen for family values, faith, and virtue was exposed as a fraud.

Over the next few hours, a picture of this man emerged that was both shocking and shameful. Although he had been a national spokesman for returning our nation to its religious roots and for allowing character and values to be taught in our schools, this man was also a well-known "player" at several large casinos. The media reported (and he himself confirmed) that he had gambled away millions of dollars at casino slot and video poker machines.

Sadly, stories involving the scandals of high profile national and religious leaders make headlines almost every week in our country. Because these leaders represent faith, values, and morality, their fall damages the very beliefs they once seemed to embody.

But the truth is, far greater damage is being caused every day in homes and churches all across our nation as professing Christians fail to live out their beliefs. They and their families attend church regularly and faithfully. Yet inside the walls of their own homes, these same families are failing and falling apart because of pride, anger, unforgiveness, immorality, and a failure to obey the faith they profess. The newspapers don't report these stories. News cameras seldom record them. But the eyes and ears of little children often witness them, and the vulnerable and impressionable minds of teenagers are forever marked by them.

It is easy for us to shake our fingers and cluck our tongues at those whose sin and hypocrisy is made public. But what would the cameras expose if they were focused on us? If they came into our homes, what would they see? If they recorded the conversations we have with our spouse and our children, what would they reveal? If they followed us to our workplace, as we ran our errands, or on a business trip, what would they witness? If they did an in-depth investigation into the entertainment we watch, the videos we rent, the websites we visit, what would they discover?

I take no joy in writing this week's introduction. In fact, it is downright painful putting these words on the page. How I wish I could be more positive and uplifting right now. But I cannot ignore what God has placed upon my heart as I have prepared the lesson this week. As Christians, our deeds are supposed to authenticate the sincerity and genuineness of our faith. Sitting in church wearing our Sunday best, we may appear to be the real deal—a model Christian. The reality, however, of our faith and commitment to Christ will be proven inside our homes, on our jobs, and as we sit alone surfing the internet.

This week your study will be intensely practical. You will be reminded of the motives and priorities to which Christ has called us. You will rediscover the importance of faith and works. You will also review some truths and scriptures that may be difficult for you to embrace—yet, I pray that you will.

In the days ahead, we will read more newspaper articles and listen to more breaking news reports involving the scandal of more prominent religious and national leaders. When we do, I pray we will be reminded that, although no camera crews are staking us out, and no reporters are writing down our every word, there is One who sees and knows our every thought, word, and deed…and one day we will all stand before Him. On that day, may He find us *faithful*.

Day One

1. As you begin another week of study, use today's Psalm as your prayer of commitment reaffirming to God your deliberate choice to follow His ways all of your days.

> *I have chosen the faithful way; I have placed*
> *Thine ordinances before me.* Psalm 119:30

2. Last week we began looking at the things Solomon instructed us to do in Ecclesiastes 3:12. His first instruction to us is to rejoice. Read Ecclesiastes 3:12, then note below Solomon's next instruction.

At this point, we could jump right in and immediately begin to look at the various ways scripture teaches us to "do good," and we'll certainly get to that in the days ahead. For today, however, your homework is designed to give you a broader perspective for "doing good" (Ecclesiastes 3:12), and it will make all the difference in the rest of your study this week.

3. Read the following verses, then complete the sentence that summarizes God's purpose for doing all that He did as He delivered Israel.

   a.   Exodus 7:17   d.   Exodus 9:14–15, 29
   b.   Exodus 8:10   e.   Exodus 10:1–2
   c.   Exodus 8:21–22

   God's purpose: that they would know _____.

4. Please read Psalm 78:1–11, then answer the following questions:

   a.   According to verse 4, *what* were the Israelites to tell to each generation?

   b.   According to verse 7–8, *why* were the Israelites to continue to tell this information to each generation?

   c.   According to verses 10–11, what happened to an earlier generation of the Israelites? What specifically did they forget?

5. Please read Psalm 96:1–5, then briefly describe why God's people are to tell others of His glory and great works.

6. Please read John 10:24–25, 30–38, and John 14:8–11. Briefly describe the purpose of the works and miracles Jesus performed.

7. Read Matthew 5:14–16, then answer the following questions:
   a.   What is our responsibility as Christians?

   b.   What is our purpose in fulfilling this responsibility?

8. As you review the passages you have studied today, what do God's works, Jesus' works, and our works all share in common?

9. You have just seen the primary purpose of good works and the reason for doing good. Yet, if we are honest, we must admit we often do good for various other reasons. List as many reasons (good and bad) as you can, regarding the motives and reasons we often have for doing good.

10. We cannot study these truths without examining our own lives. Allow the Holy Spirit to search your heart, then complete the following:
   a.   Circle the term that best describes the way in which you are proclaiming God's praise and telling others of His mighty works and deeds.

   seldom   occasionally   frequently   consistently

b. If you have children, what are some of the ways you can consistently proclaim to them the praise, mighty works, and deeds of God?

c. Recall the good things you have done over the past several days, and honestly evaluate what primarily motivated you to "do good."

Thy word is a lamp to my feet, and a light to my path.
Psalm 119:105

The unfolding of Thy words gives light.
Psalm 119:130

11. As you close your day of study today, what insights has the Lord revealed to you about your own heart? How is the Spirit leading you to apply and to respond to His word?

_____

_____

_____

_____

_____

_____

_____

_____

Day Two

1. Quiet your heart before the Lord as you prepare to study His Word. Ask Him to remind you of the mighty deeds He has performed in your life and of His goodness to you. Give Him praise and thanksgiving as you spend time alone with Him in prayer. Use today's Psalm as your response in light of all that He has done for you.

Make me walk in the path of Thy commandments, for I delight in it. Psalm 119:35

2. You will begin your lesson today by studying what Jesus taught about works and good deeds. Please read each scripture reference on the following chart, then briefly summarize what Jesus taught about works and doing good.

WHAT JESUS TAUGHT ABOUT DOING GOOD

Matthew 5:13–16
Matthew 12:33–37
Matthew 23:1–12
Luke 6:27–35
John 3:19–21
Matthew 16:27

3. What is the relationship between good deeds/works and salvation/faith? Please
    read the following scriptures and summarize what you learn.

    a.   Galatians 2:16

    b.   Ephesians 2:8–10

c. Titus 1:10–11 and 16

d. Titus 2:11–14

e. James 2:14–26

4. After having studied the relationship between good deeds/works and salvation/faith, what would you (in love) tell someone who:

a. Believes that all good people go to heaven?

b. Believes they are saved, yet their life gives no evidence of salvation?

5. Having seen the importance of good works in the life of the believer, where do we begin as we seek to "do good" (Ecclesiastes 3:12)? After all, there are endless avenues for doing good. Read Luke 10:38–42 and explain the priority Jesus taught regarding doing good.

6. Process and apply the truths you have studied today by answering the following questions:

a. In what ways do your words bear evidence of your faith? To answer this question, it may help you to recall the way you spoke and communicated before you were a Christian, after you become a Christian, and any changes or evidence you have seen since that time.

b.   In what ways do your deeds/works bear evidence of your faith? Again, it may help you to recall your life and works prior to your salvation, immediately after salvation, and any changes or evidence you have seen since that time.

c.   If you had to remove all references to your church involvement, what evidence of your faith would remain as you speak and relate to unbelievers?

d.   As you seek to give your relationship with Christ priority, what obstacles often draw you away from seeking Him first in this season of your life? How can you relate to Martha?

Insights   7.   Take a few minutes to record any insights the Holy Spirit has given you today and the ways in which you believe He would have you apply them to your life.

Thy word is a lamp to my feet, and a light to my path.
Psalm 119:105

The unfolding of Thy words gives light.
Psalm 119:130

Day Three

1. The goal of all Bible study is to know God more intimately and to apply His Word practically to our lives through the power of His Spirit. As you have been seeing that goal realized in your own life, profess today's Psalm to the Lord and ask him to continue to teach and transform you through the power of His Word.

This has become mine, that
I observe Thy precepts. Psalm 119:56

2. Begin your study today by reviewing questions 7–8 from Day One of this lesson.

3. Please summarize what our primary purpose and motive should be in all that we do?

4. In Day One, we learned the motivation for doing good. In Day Two, we learned what Jesus taught about works and good deeds as well as the relationship between faith and good works. Today we need to focus on how we are enabled and equipped to "do good" (Ecclesiastes 3:12) in word and in deed. Just as there are right and wrong motivations for doing good, there are right and wrong ways to do good. In the following chart, read the scripture references listed, then briefly summarize what you learn about the right and wrong ways to do good.

PLEASE NOTE: Some references may give the right way, others may reveal the wrong way, and some may give both.

THE RIGHT WAY TO DO GOOD	THE WRONG WAY TO DO GOOD
Micah 6:8	
Matthew 23:5	

The Right Way to Do Good	The Wrong Way to Do Good
2 Corinthians 9:8	
Galatians 5:16, 22–25	
Philippians 2:3–8	
James 2:1–9	
James 3:13–14	

5. God empowers us by His grace and through His Spirit to do good works. But there are also several things God uses to equip us as we serve Him. Please read the following scriptures, and briefly describe those things God uses to equip us for service:

   a.   Ephesians 4:11–12

      b.   Colossians 1:29

      c.   2 Timothy 3:16–17

      d.   Hebrews 10:24–25

6. In the book of Revelation, Christ speaks to seven churches. These were literal churches in the early days of church history, but these messages continue to apply to the church today as well as to individual believers. Jesus has much to say about the importance of "deeds" in these messages, but He also reveals that good deeds alone cannot attain His full blessing and reward. Please read excerpts from some of Christ's messages to the churches, and note what He desires to see in our lives in addition to good deeds.

      a.   Revelation 2:1–5

      b.   Revelation 2:18–20

      c.   Revelation 3:1–3

      d.   Revelation 3:14–17

7. Finally, how has the Lord spoken to your heart today through your study? Please record any insights He has revealed to you.

Thy word is a lamp to my feet, and a light to my path.
Psalm 119:105

The unfolding of Thy words gives light.
Psalm 119:130

_____

_____

_____

_____

_____

_____

_____

_____

Day Four

1. Please take a few moments to pray before you begin your study. Ask God to reveal any areas in your life where you are hesitating to obey Him. It may be fear, pride, or a sin that continually defeats you. It may also be a step of faith He is clearly leading you to take, even though you are unsure of the consequences. Is there any hesitancy in your obedience to Him? If so, confess and repent of it today. Then quickly and without delay, fully obey Him.

    I hastened and did not delay to keep Thy commandments. Psalm 119:60

    As we continue our study on how to "do good" (Ecclesiastes 3:12) in every season of our lives, our focus today will be specifically geared to women. We will be studying only those passages that give instructions to women. Some of these passages will refer to married women, and others will refer to mothers. Several passages are practical for all women. Whether or not you are married, have children, or are a widow, please study each passage. Even if some of the passages do not apply to you in this season of your life, they may apply to you in a future season. And because our culture has become so gender neutral and opposed to acknowledging any differences between men and women, this study from God's timeless, unchanging Word will reacquaint us with God's perspective regarding women's roles and responsibilities.

2. Please read the scriptures in each of the charts on the following pages. In the center column, briefly summarize how it should be applied. In the final column, circle whether or not this instruction or responsibility applies to you in your current season. Please feel free to use any commentaries or Bible reference books you may have in order to gain a greater depth of understanding. Or go online and use Bible commentary sources (such as www.bibleclassics.com, www.biblegateway.com, and www.studylight.org) to research these scriptures.

There is a Season

DOING GOOD AS A WOMAN

Reference	As a woman, I am to...	Applies to Current Season?	
Matthew 15:3–6		Yes	No
1 Timothy 2:9–10		Yes	No
Titus 2:3–5		Yes	No

DOING GOOD AS A MOTHER

Reference	As a mother, I am to...	Applies to Current Season?	
Deut. 6:4–7		Yes	No
Proverbs 19:18		Yes	No
Proverbs 22:6		Yes	No
Proverbs 31:14–15, 21, 26–27		Yes	No

DOING GOOD AS A WIFE

Reference	As a wife, I am to...	Applies to Current Season?	
Genesis 2:18		Yes	No
Proverbs 31:11–12		Yes	No
1 Cor, 7:3–5		Yes	No
1 Cor. 7:10–15		Yes	No
1 Cor. 14:34–35		Yes	No
Ephesians 5:22–24, 33		Yes	No
1 Peter 3:1–4		Yes	No

3. As you compiled your chart, were there any problems or questions you had regarding what you studied? If so, please list them.

4. Review your chart asking the Lord to reveal any hesitancy you may have in obeying these instructions and in fulfilling these responsibilities. On your chart, circle any reference(s) the Lord used to speak to you. Describe the way you believe God is leading you to respond to these specific scriptures.

Thy word is a lamp to my feet, and a light to my path.
Psalm 119:105

The unfolding of Thy words gives light.
Psalm 119:130

Insights

5. Please record any insights the Lord has given you today as you have spent time in His Word.

_____

_____

_____

_____

_____

_____

_____

_____

Day Five

1. Let the words of today's Psalm be the sincere desire of your heart and the prayer of your lips.

> *Establish my footsteps in Thy word, and do not let any iniquity have dominion over me.* Psalm 119:133

On this final day of our lesson, we will focus on how to "do good" (Ecclesiastes 3:12) to others. Many of the scriptures you have studied earlier in this week's lesson would also apply to the study today. However, we will limit our focus today to references you have not yet studied.

2. Read the scriptures on the following chart. Describe who we're to do good to and briefly summarize how we're to do good.

DOING GOOD TO OTHERS

Reference	Do Good To...	Do Good By...
Proverbs 3:27–28		
Proverbs 31:20		
Isaiah 1:17		
Romans 12:21		
1 Cor. 12:1, 4–7, 1 Peter 4:10		
1 Timothy 6:17–18		

3. Acts 9:36–42 is the inspiring account of a woman who was used in a mighty way during the days of the early church. She is a beautiful example of servanthood. Please read this account, then answer the following questions:

   a. According to verse 36, what was this woman's name, and how was she described?

   b. According to verse 37, what happened to her?

   c. How did her friends respond in verses 38–39?

   d. What does the response of her friends in verses 38–39 reveal to you about her life and influence and how others felt about her?

   e. In addition to what you learned from verse 36, how else did God choose to use this woman?

   f. You probably know other women like Dorcas whose lives and service have made an impact upon your life and the lives of others. List a few names of some of the women you have known throughout your life who are very much like Dorcas, then take a few moments to thank the Lord for them.

   g. Now do something very practical that will be a wonderful encouragement to one of the significant women for whom you just prayed. Write one of them a note, and thank them for the blessing and inspiration they have been in your life. Women like Dorcas are rare, and they are seldom in the limelight. Often, their service goes unrecognized, and *they* do not seek recognition. That is why a simple note expressing your appreciation will be even more meaningful. You do not need fancy stationery, just use whatever you have. Do not delay. Let them know today of your gratitude for the way you have seen God glorified through their life.

4. Two final scriptures are given to encourage you as you seek to live out the principles you have studied this week. Please read the following scriptures, then describe how they encourage you.

   a.   Galatians 6:9–10

   b.   1 Corinthians 15:58

5. Finally, conclude your time of study this week by journaling. Simply and honestly write out the things that come to your mind as you reflect upon the way the Lord has spoken to you this week and the way it has impacted your life.

My Journal

THIS WEEK THE LORD…

_____
_____
_____
_____
_____
_____
_____
_____
_____

AS A RESULT, I…

_____
_____
_____
_____
_____
_____
_____
_____
_____
_____

You have spent a very serious week in God's Word. God bless you, dear sister, for all of the scriptures you've looked up and read and read and re-read and summarized on chart after chart after chart! When you complete this study, I'm hoping the pages of your Bible are a little more worn, that many more of its verses have been underlined and committed to memory and that, perhaps, a few of its pages even bear tear stains because of the way God moved in your heart as you read the words He penned to you.

I love a good Jane Austen novel, and Agatha Christie's murder mysteries used to be some of my favorite reading. Several of Jane Austen's books have been adapted into movies, and I've enjoyed watching them. But the film versions are usually fairly faithful to the original stories. Occasionally, I've re-read some of my old Agatha Christie mysteries, but they're no longer mysteries—they always turn out just like they did the first time I read them.

But when I read the Word, it is new, it is fresh. Its message is deeper and its words are richer each time I open its pages. No book ever written captivates, stimulates, and motivates me like God's Word does. If I live to be one hundred, and if I am able to find a strong enough pair of glasses to read with, I believe God's Word will still speak to my old heart in brand new ways!

How I pray—

even though His Word may have broken
your heart with its convicting power,

even though its instructions may have
challenged you with the unwavering command
that calls you to take up your cross daily, and

even though it requires both your
time and your diligence to correctly
interpret and to faithfully apply it—

that you are witnessing the transforming, renewing work it is doing in your life and above all, that you are falling in love with its Author over and over again as you "grow in the grace and knowledge" (2 Peter 3:18) of His lavish love for you!

I will close now with a statement that I believe with my whole heart. Here it is: There is nothing sadder than an old Bible that looks brand new. Sister, let's wear out our Bibles!

Doing Good in Every Season

I. Review

A. In Ecclesiastes, Solomon's search for meaning in life is ultimately a search for

_____ / _____ in life.

B. In Ecclesiastes 3:12–14, we see three _____ that will enable us to experience joy, meaning, and contentment in every season of our lives.

C. In this study, we are calling these _____, the _____.

1. Door # 1 = _____

   Focus on _____

2. Door # 2 = _____

   Focus on _____

II. Scripture teaches we are to...

A. Do good in our _____. *Ecc. 3:12*

B. Do good with all of your _____. *Ecc. 9:10*

C. Do good to all _____ and especially to other Christians. *Gal. 6:10*

D. Do good as _____ rather than _____. *Col. 3:23*

E. Do good so that _____ will see your _____ and _____ God. *Matt. 5:14-16*

III. Questions and Answers—*Matt. 25:14–29, 1 Cor. 3:11–15*

Q. What are the seven words every Christian longs to hear?

A. _____

Q. Who will hear these words?

A. _____

Q. How will we be judged?

A. _____

Q. What will be the outcome of the judgment?

A. **We will receive** _____ **or we will** _____ _____, **but we cannot** _____.

IV.   Role Models Who Will Hear, "Well Done"

A.   _____—*Acts 9:36–42*

- she was _____.

- she served the Lord by serving others _____.

B.   _____—*Rom. 16:1–2*

- she was a _____ of the church.

- she was a _____ of many, and of _____ as well.

C.   _____ and _____—*Rom. 16:3–5, Acts 18:18–28*

- fellow _____ in Christ Jesus.

- their _____ was used as a _____—good stewards.

D.   _____, _____, _____, and _____—
Rom. 16:6 and 12

- all of these were _____.

- all of these shared this in common: they _____ _____ for the Lord.

E.   _____ mother—*Rom. 16:13, Mark 15:20–21*

- ministered to Paul as a _____.

- her background: Jewish from _____ / _____.

- her husband: _____, who helped _____ Jesus' _____.

- her _____ and _____ to Paul was an extension
of her _____ for Christ.

*Door # 2: Doing good...*_____

Seeing Good in Every Season

Several years ago, we purchased a new minivan. It had been ten years since we had owned a new family car, and we were so excited about all of the up-to-date features on our new car. Naturally, one of the very first things my teenage sons wanted to do was to check out the new car stereo—and to program the radio to their stations. Notice I said their stations, not my stations.

Programming the car radio appeared, at first, to be a potential power struggle. But just as the tension between my teenage sons and my old-fogey self began to swell, just as we began to take sides and passionately present our arguments, we discovered to our surprise and delight that our new car possessed an amazing feature—a feature that had the power to bridge the enormous gap between the generations in our family! We discovered our new car came equipped with twice as many FM radio presets as our old model had. Hallelujah! Revival broke out in the Cole minivan that day! I could program the radio with my stations, and the teenagers could program the radio with their stations. It appeared we would all drive happily ever after. Alas, it was not to be.

You see, there was one small but critical problem we had not considered. One of these teenage sons was already a full-fledged, license-carrying driver, and the other teenage son soon would be, too. These were young men who, at times, would be driving this minivan—without their middle-aged mother. Now these young men of mine were very cautious when they borrowed my car. They would occasionally take it for short trips, and they would return the car in the same condition as it had been before they had driven it—or so it appeared. What I could not know was that as my car sat waiting in the garage for me, it held a kind of "bomb" that was just waiting to go off the next day when I would turn its key!

If you have ever had teenagers who have borrowed your car, you know very well the deafening "bomb" that often explodes when the next driver innocently starts the ignition. The engine turns over and instantaneously, without warning, the "bomb" goes off—the deafening noise of so-called music blaring at full volume from a radio station that was definitely not preset by the middle-aged car owner. Needless to say, I have experienced the nerve-wracking shell shock of that explosion many times.

These days, my youngest son is driving the minivan—with a learner's permit, which means I am sitting in the front seat beside him (in that slightly stiffened parent-of-a-brand-new-driver position). When he punches the buttons on the radio or CD player, I recognize instantly we are no longer listening to *my* music, we're listening to *his* music.

As the mother of teenage drivers, one of the ways I've been able to discern where they are spiritually is through those revealing radio preset buttons in my car—and in more recent years, in their own cars. Sometimes the information those preset channels have revealed has made me get on my knees and pray for their spiritual well being. At other times, it has made me rejoice as I've listened to the lyrics of contemporary Christian music reverberating from the stereo inside their car. You can tell a lot about a teenager (and an adult as well) by the preset stations on their car radio.

Although it may sound strange, I believe our minds are a lot like car radios. Each day, dozens of times per day, we punch the preset buttons of our minds and listen to the thoughts being played on the channels of our mind. Just like we have favorite stations preset in our car radios, we also have favorite preset thoughts we think. If our inmost thoughts are true, honorable, right, and pure (Philippians 4:8), our external lives will reveal it. But if the channels we listen to are bitter, corrupt, slanderous, and impure, our lives will reflect that as well. One of the truest ways you and I can know whether we're progressing or regressing spiritually is by the thoughts we purposefully "play."

This week you will be examining the way you think and the way your thoughts affect the other aspects of your life. You will also be studying how you view this season of your life and whether or not you have accepted God's gift: enjoying the life He's given you. Some of us are way too serious and task-oriented. In all of our productivity and busyness, we have forgotten that God has "richly (supplied) us with all things to enjoy" (1 Timothy 6:17). Hopefully, this week's lesson will serve as a reminder of that.

What do your current thoughts reveal about your own spiritual condition? Is it time for you to reprogram the preset buttons in your mind? Are you *enjoying* this present season of your life, or are you *enduring* it? Maybe it's time for you to lighten up a little and enjoy life—especially those of you who are parents of teenager drivers. In fact, I think I'll dedicate this week's lesson to the parents of teenage drivers everywhere!

Day One

1. Spend some time in prayer as you begin your study this week. Use today's Psalm to thank God for the way He has faithfully used His Word to encourage and strengthen you through the seasons of your life. Recount to God specific occasions when He lovingly delivered you, healed you, or sustained you through challenging, difficult days.

> *If Thy Law had not been my delight, then I would have perished in my affliction.* Psalm 119:92

2. Begin your study by reading and reviewing the familiar verses listed below.

> *There is an appointed time ('a season' KJV) for everything, and there is a time for every event under heaven... He has made everything appropriate in its time. He has also set eternity in their heart, yet so that man will not find out the work which God has done from the beginning even to the end.* Ecclesiastes 3:1 and 11

In Week 6, you learned these two verses contain four truths about life. These four truths are partially listed on the following page. Please review them by filling in each blank. (If you need help, you may turn to page 108 in your homework where these truths were first given to you.)

Four Truths About Life

1) There is a _____ for _____ in life.

2) God has made everything _____ , appropriate, and with _____ in its time.

3) God has made us long for _____ significance and meaning in our lives.

4) We cannot yet fully _____ the _____ significance, value, and purpose of our lives.

3. After Solomon states these four truths about life, he then reveals how we are to live in light of these truths. Please read and review the following verse.

> *I know that there is nothing better for them than to rejoice, and do good in one's lifetime.* Ecclesiastes 3:12

According to this verse, what two things are we encouraged to do throughout our lifetime?

4. Our focus this week will be on Solomon's next exhortation. Please read the following verse. **NOTE: Two translations of this verse have been given so that you may have a greater understanding of the specific exhortation we will be studying this week.**

> *Moreover, that every man who eats and drinks sees good in all his labor—it is the gift of God.* Ecclesiastes 3:13 (NAS)

> *And also that every man should eat and drink, and enjoy the good of all his labour, it is the gift of God.* Ecclesiastes 3:13 (KJV)

As you can see, Solomon's third exhortation is somewhat different in each translation. Compare each translation by filling in the blanks below, then meditate on each phrase.

a. NAS: _____ good in _____ his _____

b. KJV: _____ the good of _____ his _____

5. The words "sees" (NAS) and "enjoy" (KJV) are translated from the Hebrew the word "raah" and re-defined as follows:

a. ***Strong's Concordance:*** to *see,* lit. or fig. (in numerous applications…), advise self…(make to) enjoy, have experience…think, view.[17]

b. ***The Complete Word Study Old Testament:*** to see; to see intellectually, to look; …to view…regard; to perceive…to experience…to enjoy.[18]

6. The word "good" (NAS and KJV) is translated from the Hebrew word "towb" or "tov" and is defined as follows:

   a. ***Strong's Concordance:*** *good*…in the widest sense.[19]

   b. ***The Complete Word Study Old Testament:*** It means good, pleasant, beautiful, excellent, lovely, delightful…joyful…; the good, the right, virtue, happiness, pleasantness. It may refer to practical or economic benefits…aesthetic or sensual goodness.[20]

7. Now, in your own words, describe what you believe the exhortation "sees good" (NAS), and "enjoy the good" (KJV) means. In other words, how would you practically apply this exhortation in your everyday life?

8. The following scriptures from Ecclesiastes may give you further insight into the meaning of Ecclesiastes 3:12. Please read them, then make notes of your insights (especially notice any additional areas of life we are exhorted to enjoy beyond our labor).

   a. Ecclesiastes 2:24–26

   b. Ecclesiastes 5:18

   c. Ecclesiastes 9:9

9. According to Ecclesiastes 3:13 and to the additional verses you just read, why are we to "see good" (NAS) or to "enjoy good" (KJV)?

10. In this current season of your life, what is your primary work or labor? List below what an average week of labor involves for you.

11. Honestly describe how you view your work or your labor in this season of your life.

12. Under the headings below, list the things you most and least enjoy doing in this season of your life. Do not limit this list to tasks and responsibilities. Please add any hobbies or other things you enjoy.

I Most Enjoy Doing	I Least Enjoy Doing

13. As you look at the list of things you least enjoy doing, is it possible to view any of these things as good? (It may help to review the definitions you were given earlier in item number 6.) If so, describe the good in these tasks.

14. Before you close your workbook today, take a few moments to record the way in which the Holy Spirit has spoken to your heart. What has He revealed to you today?

_____

_____

_____

_____

_____

_____

_____

Day Two

1. Bow your head in prayer and submit yourself and your time of study to the Lord. Profess to Him the truths of today's Psalm, and ask Him to remind you continually to keep your thoughts centered on Him.

> *O how I love Thy law! It is my
> meditation all the day.* Psalm 119:97

2. Yesterday you studied Ecclesiastes 3:13 and Solomon's exhortation to "(see) good in all of (our) labor" (NAS), or to "enjoy the good of all of (our) labour" (KJV). This verse may be interpreted in various ways. The two interpretations we will focus on are these:

   a. We are exhorted to view our life and labor as good.
   b. We are exhorted to experience enjoyment in our life and labor.

   The first interpretation involves our attitude toward our life and labor. The second interpretation involves our experience in our life and labor.

   You also saw the reason we are exhorted to "(see) good" (NAS), and to "enjoy the good of all of (our) labour" (KJV). Ecclesiastes 3:13 says that the ability to view and to enjoy our life and labor is "the gift of God" (NAS). In other words, God's gift to us and His desire for us is that we view our life and labor as good, and that we enjoy our life and labor in every season of our lives.

3. In order to reinforce the truths you have just reviewed, please read the following scriptures, then note what you learn from them:

   a. John 10:10

   b. 1 Timothy 6:17b

4. Review the four truths about life found in Ecclesiastes 3:1 and 11 (you completed a list of these truths in your homework yesterday in question 2). In light of these truths, what is also true about your life and labor in every season of your life?

As you think about all that you have studied yesterday and today, please consider the following questions:

- What is your attitude toward your life and work in this divinely appointed season of your life?
- Are you experiencing enjoyment in your life and labor in this divinely appointed season of your life?

The two questions above will be the focus of your study for the remainder of this week. Today you will begin focusing on the first question by studying what scripture teaches about the mind, attitude, and thought life of the believer.

5. Begin your study on the mind/heart/attitude by reading the following scriptures, then briefly summarize what you learn from them:

   a. Psalm 139:1–4

   b. Proverbs 3:5–6

   c. Proverbs 4:23

   d. Proverbs 23:7a

6. Read the following scriptures, then note what you learn about the relationship between the heart/mind and our words/deeds, and the importance of "(seeing) good" (Ecclesiastes 3:13).

   a. Psalm 37:1–8

      b.   Proverbs 15:28

      c.   Matthew 15:10–11, 17–20

      d.   Luke 6:45

7.   You have just studied several scriptures that reveal the relationship between our thoughts and our deeds. In Psalm 73, Asaph (a Levite who also was a musician, poet, and prophet) reveals how his thoughts affected him and almost caused him to stumble. Please read this Psalm noting the repeated pronouns "they," "their," and "them," as well as Asaph's references to himself. After you have finished reading this Psalm, please answer the following questions:

      a.   According to verses 2–3, what almost caused Asaph to stumble?

      b.   What was the focus of Asaph's thoughts in verses 3–14?

      c.   Even in Asaph's negative state of mind, what was he careful not to do (verse 15)?

      d.   According to verses 16 and 21–22 what was the result of Asaph's negative, consuming thoughts?

e.   How did Asaph find peace? How did Asaph "(see) good" (Ecclesiastes 3:13)? List the verses that reveal the answer to these questions and summarize their content.

8. Jeremiah is another biblical character who responds to his season of despair by crying out to God. Lamentations 3 records some of the most raw, honest words found in scripture as Jeremiah pours out his heart to God. If you have ever been in a deep, hopeless pit of despair or depression, you will likely relate to Jeremiah. Please read Lamentations 3:1–18, then answer the following:

a.   How does Jeremiah describe himself in verse 1a, and who has caused his present pain according to verse 1b?

b.   Using verses 2–17, record some of Jeremiah's own words that express what he has experienced and how he honestly feels.

c.   According to verse 18, Jeremiah's "strength has perished," but what else has also perished?

d.   In verse 21, Jeremiah turns a corner in his thoughts—he "sees good" (Ecclesiastes 3:13). Please read verses 21–25, and note what Jeremiah "recalls to mind," and the result he then experiences.

e.   According to this passage, how is it possible for hope to be restored when all hope seems to have perished?

9.   Reflect back over the past few days of your life. Have you allowed yourself recently to become mentally consumed by negative thoughts about your life, your labor, your circumstances, or other people? If so, describe that experience, your specific thoughts, and how your thoughts affected you mentally, emotionally, physically, and spiritually. Be as honest as Asaph was.

10. Have you ever experienced a season of hopelessness, despair, or depression? If so, describe that experience, your thoughts in the midst of that season, and how you responded. Be as honest as Jeremiah was.

One of the most beautiful and amazing things we see in both Asaph and Jeremiah's writings is their honesty and openness before God. These men did not "vent" their frustrations to everyone who crossed their path (as we are often prone to do). Instead, they "vented" their innermost thoughts to God, and they held nothing back from Him. As you saw in Psalm 139, He knows our thoughts even before we think them—all the more reason we can safely bring them before Him. I encourage you today, if you're hurting, disappointed, bitter, unhappy, depressed, or even fuming mad, spend some extended time with the Lord in prayer. Pour it all out before Him. Then, take a deep breath, and turn your thoughts solely upon Him—"(see) good" (Ecclesiastes 3:13)—and read the words from Lamentations 3:21–25 aloud to the Lord in whom you hope.

Insights

11. How has the Lord spoken to you today as you have studied what His Word says about your heart, mind, attitude, and thoughts? Are there any specific areas in your life or in your labor in which you need to "(see) good" (Ecclesiastes 3:13)?

Thy word is a lamp to my feet, and a light to my path.
Psalm 119:105

The unfolding of Thy words gives light.
Psalm 119:130

_____

_____

_____

_____

_____

_____

_____

_____

_____

Day Three

1. As you can see in today's Psalm, trouble and anguish are certainly a part of this life, but God's Word has given us light, hope, and promise in every season. Spend time in prayer before you begin your study, and if your heart is troubled about anything, bring it before the Lord today. Ask Him to give you hope as you focus on Him.

Pray

Trouble and anguish have come upon me; yet Thy commandments are my delight. Psalm 119:143

Keeping our thoughts and attitudes pure is something we all struggle with. As long as we live in these fleshly bodies, we will always experience a war within—a conflict between our flesh and our redeemed heart and mind. But as Christians, we have the ability to access the power of the Holy Spirit which means we can win the daily battle for control of our thoughts and minds. That's the wonderful news you're going to study today.

There is a Season

2. Please read the scriptures on the following chart, then summarize the instructions they teach regarding how you can win the battle within.

WINNING THE BATTLE WITHIN

Romans 6:11–13
Romans 12:1–2
1 Corinthians 13:11—**NOTE: Think about this verse; specifically, how do children reason and think?**
2 Corinthians 10:3–5

WINNING THE BATTLE WITHIN

Ephesians 4:17–24
Ephesians 6:10–18

3. In the introduction to this lesson, you read that our minds are often like car radios with buttons we have preset to the stations we listen to most. Honestly describe what "stations" you listen to most within your mind. In other words, what thoughts do you most frequently entertain? Try to remember what your mind is most consumed with on a typical day. What are the "stations" you most frequently play within your mind? (Examples of some of these stations might be the "I'm so worried about my kids" station, or the "My husband is driving me crazy" station, or the "I hate this job" station.)

4. To help you "reset the buttons on the radio of your mind," please read the following scriptures, and describe the "stations" they instruct you to preset within your mind so that you may "(see) good" according to Ecclesiastes 3:13.

   a.   Matthew 22:37

   b.   Philippians 4:6–8

   c.   Colossians 3:1–3

I highly encourage you to memorize the scriptures above so you can quickly change the station of your mind by using them to direct and correct your thoughts. Preset His Word within your heart through consistent study and scripture memorization. When your flesh or your enemy begin to play their favorite stations, you will then be able to quickly punch a scripture station you've memorized to destroy those "speculations and…lofty thing(s) raised up against the knowledge of God," and you will effectively be able to take "every thought captive to the obedience of Christ" (2 Corinthians 10:5).

Thy word is a lamp to my feet, and a light to my path.
Psalm 119:105

The unfolding of Thy words gives light.
Psalm 119:130

Insights

5. Conclude your time of study today by evaluating how the Lord has spoken to you. Please write your insights below.

_____

_____

_____

_____

_____

_____

_____

_____

Day Four

1. Begin your day of study in prayer and praise. Ask the Lord to prompt and remind you to praise Him, as the psalmist did, throughout your entire day.

> *Seven times a day I praise You for Your*
> *righteous laws.* Psalm 119:164 (NIV)

Today you will begin to focus on evaluating the "enjoyment factor" in your life. As you saw in Day One, the King James Version translates Ecclesiastes 3:13 as follows:

> *And also that every man should eat and drink, and enjoy the*
> *good of all his labour, it is the gift of God.* Ecclesiastes 3:13 (KJV)

This verse may cause you to ask: Am I experiencing enjoyment in my life and labor in this divinely appointed season of my life?

2. Before you begin your study of scripture, please answer the following question: What are some of the reasons we often fail to enjoy our life and our labor? (Example: busyness, etc.) Please compile a brief list of some common answers to this question.

3. Describe the most enjoyable past season of your life. What made that season so enjoyable?

4. Describe the "enjoyment factor" of your current season. How does it compare or contrast with the season you previously described? Why do you think it is more or less enjoyable than the season you previously described?

5. If you qualify as a senior adult, why do you think younger women often fail to enjoy life? With the wisdom you have now gained, how would you specifically encourage women to enjoy their life and their labor?

6. Jesus desires for us to experience His joy, which indicates He was joyful and that He enjoyed His life and labor. What were the rhythms of His life like? What was His routine? Take a quick look at each reference listed below. Try to follow Christ vicariously in order to understand His schedule, His habits, and His way of life. If you have a map of Israel (in the time of Christ) in your Bible, it would be helpful to chart Jesus' course as you read.

   a. John 2:1–16, 23 (Notice it is Passover)

   b. John 3:1–3, 22

   c. John 4:1–10, 25–40, 43, 46–50

   d. John 5:1–2, 5–6, 8–10, 18–20, 30

   e. John 6:1–4, 10–15 (Notice the reference to Passover in verse 4 again.)

   This is just a thumbnail sketch from one of the gospels concerning one year in Jesus' life and ministry. From what you observed, please answer the following questions.

   f. How would you describe Jesus' schedule?

   g. How did Jesus determine his schedule and His labor/ministry?

h.   As Jesus traveled to the various cities in which He ministered, how did He typically travel? How would this have affected Him, and what opportunities would it have provided him?

i.   How did Jesus handle those who were not pleased with His life and ministry?

7.   Examine just a few more scriptures from Mark that reveal another facet of Jesus' schedule. Please read them, then describe what they reveal about Jesus, His life, and His labor.

a.   Mark 1:32–39

b.   Mark 6:30–32

c.   Mark 6:42–46

8. What principles did you learn from Jesus' life that would enable you to enjoy your life and labor in a more satisfying way?

Thy word is a lamp to my feet, and a light to my path.
Psalm 119:105

The unfolding of Thy words gives light.
Psalm 119:130

9. Has the Lord given you any insights that you believe He would have you apply to your life, labor, and schedule? If so, please make notes of your insights in the space provided below.

_____

_____

_____

_____

_____

_____

_____

_____

Day Five

1. As you begin your final day of study this week, thank God for the peace and assurance He has given you through His Word.

   Those who love Thy laws have great peace, and nothing causes them to stumble. Psalm 119:165

   Today your study will be very brief. The greater part of our time will be spent evaluating your schedule so that you can receive the gift God has given you: to "enjoy good" (Ecclesiastes 3:13).

2. Review the pages of your study this week. Ask the Lord to enable you to see any specific scriptures or principles He is leading you to apply to a specific area of your life or labor.

3. You only have one new passage to study today. Please read Ephesians 5:15–17, then answer the following questions:

    a.   What is the instruction concerning time in this verse?

    b.   How does this verse apply to the exhortation you studied from Ecclesiastes 3:13?

    c.   How would this verse apply to the topic of our study: the seasons of life?

4. This week our study has focused on Ecclesiastes 3:13 and the following two questions this scripture has caused us to ask:

    • What is your attitude toward your life and work in this divinely appointed season of your life?
    • Are you experiencing enjoyment in your life and labor in this divinely appointed season of your life?

Today you will be doing a personal evaluation of your life and labor. On the following pages, three charts have been provided to help you in this evaluation. Instructions for each chart also are provided.

The goal of this assignment is to help you apply the truths you have learned this week. Ask the Lord to reveal the specific ways you are to apply what He has taught you in your relationships, responsibilities, and recreation. Ask Him to give you wisdom concerning your present season and to reveal any areas in which you may be over-committed—or lack commitment.

PRIORITY RELATIONSHIPS CHART

1) List the names of your priority relationships in the first column in order of their priority (if you have children, order them according to their age, listing the oldest child first). These may include any family, relatives, friends, colleagues, etc. that you consider to be priority relationships.
   NOTE: God has already been given first place on your chart.
2) In the next column, rate your relationships with this person using the following scale:
   1 = poor   2 = average   3 = good
3) In the next two columns, place a checkmark if your attitude or enjoyment level in this relationship needs improvement.
4) In the final column, list any specific ways you could improve this relationship.

Names	Rating	Needs Improved Attitude	Needs Improved Enjoyment	I could improve by:
God				

PRIMARY RESPONSIBILITIES CHART

1) List in order of their priority, your personal responsibilities in this season of your life. (Example: housework, meal planning and preparation, career/job, church responsibilities, etc.)

2) In the next column, rate the quality of your labor using the same scale you used to rate your relationships:

1 = poor   2 = average   3 = good

3) In the next two columns, place a checkmark if your attitude or enjoyment level in this labor needs improvement.

4) In the final column, list any specific ways you could improve your labor. (Example: adjust schedule, delegate, etc.)

My Responsibility	Rating	Needs Improved Attitude	Needs Improved Enjoyment	Ideas for improvement

There is a Season

RECREATION & ENJOYABLE ACTIVITIES

1) List, in order of their enjoyment level, the things you personally enjoy doing now, or would like to do in a future season. (Example: gardening, exercise, scrapbooking, theatre, etc.)

2) In the next column, place a checkmark if this activity is something you are able to enjoy now (in this season of your life) or desire later (in a future season of life).

3) If you are married and/or if you have children, complete the other sections by determining activities you and your spouse and/or you and your children enjoy. Place a checkmark in those boxes denoting whether this is something you would be able to enjoy with them now or in a future season.

	Activities	Enjoy Now	Enjoy Later
Personal			
With My Mate			
Family Activities			

5. Find your home calendar or your own daily organizer. Take a few minutes to apply the work you have done on your charts today. Schedule some time for enjoyable, replenishing activities by yourself, with your spouse, with your children, and with your friends and relatives. If you do not schedule and plan these days, you will miss so many opportunities to enjoy your life *and* to enjoy those whom you love most. Remember, enjoyment is God's gift and reward to you.

6. Conclude your week of study by journaling. Using your journal page, summarize the principles and scriptures God has used in your life this week. Are you viewing your life and labor as a good gift from the hand of God? Are you enjoying the blessings God has so richly given you in this brief season of your life? How will you respond to God's Word this week?

My Journal

THIS WEEK THE LORD...

_____
_____
_____
_____
_____
_____
_____
_____
_____

AS A RESULT, I...

_____
_____
_____
_____
_____
_____
_____
_____
_____

One of the most enjoyable things I've experienced in this season of my life has been in my relationship with my husband, Bill. Something happened a few years ago when our boys began driving—we rediscovered one another. Now that's one positive aspect of having teenage drivers!

As our sons became increasingly mobile, they were constantly on-the-go with their friends. At first, it felt strange…just the two of us going out to dinner together…just the two of us in the car together…just the two of us alone in an empty house together. But you know what—we're getting used to it!

In this season of our life, for a few days each summer around our anniversary date, we usually take a car trip to our favorite place: the Texas Hill Country. And somewhere along the way on one of those trips, Bill and I unexpectedly developed a hobby together. We began stopping in small-town antique stores and meddling around, and we discovered we enjoy "antiquing." For us, it is replenishing, relaxing, and simply enjoyable to spend the day together just rummaging through a little out-of-the-way, off-the-beaten-path antique store.

Bill and I will celebrate our twenty-fifth anniversary this year, and we are enjoying our life together now more than we ever have. Previous seasons of our marriage have been wonderful and sweet, busy and harried, but I believe our best and most enjoyable years together are still ahead of us.

Our baby, J.J., is fifteen. When he leaves for college, I'll grieve, and I'll probably shed buckets of tears. But I know this—should God bless Bill and me with five or twenty-five more years of marriage, I will recognize each year as God's gift to us, and I will "Enjoy life with the (man) whom (I) love all the days of (my)…life which He has given to (me) under the sun" (Ecclesiastes 9:9).

Dear sister, whatever *your* season, whatever *your* life and labor—embrace and enjoy it—it is God's gift to you.

Seeing Good in Every Season

I. Principles of Contentment

    A. _____ to the _____ _____ about life. *Ecc. 3:1–11*

    B. _____ the _____. *Ecc. 3:12–13*

        1. Door # 1 = _____ : _____ God.

        2. Door # 2 = _____ : _____ others.

        3. Door # 3 = _____ / _____ : Focus on our attitude and our experiences.

II. Scripture teaches we are to…

    A. See good and enjoy the good of both our _____ and our _____. *Ecc. 2:24, 3:13*

    B. Enjoy life with _____ we _____ . *Ecc. 9:9*

    C. Recognize our life, labor, and our _____ _____ are a _____ and _____ from God. *Ecc. 2:24, 3:13, 5:18, 9:9*

III. Enjoying your life and labor:

Principles to Practice

    1. Keep your _____ God's _____. *Matt. 6:31–34.*

    2. _____ in the _____ . *Ps. 37:4, 90:14, 100:2, 16:11*

    3. Stop _____ about everything and start _____ about everything. *Phil. 4:6–8*

    4. _____ your _____ often. *Ps. 103:1–14*

    5. Recognize your _____ and accept its _____ , and embrace its _____ . *Ecc. 3:1–8*

    6. _____ your schedule and your _____ . *2 Cor. 11:3*

    7. Stop trying to _____ _____ . *Luke 4:14–30*

8. Make the _____ a regular part of your life: _____, _____, and

_____. *Gen. 2:1–3, 1 Tim. 6:17*

9. Purposefully plan and schedule _____. *Ecc. 3:4*

10. Practice _____. *Rom. 12:10a, 13b*

The Key to Contentment

Fear is a word with a very negative connotation. It dominates the headlines almost daily. Fear and its evil companion, terror, have escalated in recent years, and the unsettling reality is that fear and terror no longer limit themselves to continents beyond our shores. Fear and terror have descended upon our very own soil.

Lately, I have been reading the inspirational Old Testament book of Nehemiah. Nehemiah was the man God used to rebuild the wall around Jerusalem after it had been torn down and its gates had been burned by the Babylonian army, a century before Nehemiah was even born. God allowed the Babylonians to be His instrument of judgment upon Israel because His people had disobeyed and forgotten Him. They had embraced the idolatry of the nations surrounding them, so God used the pagan armies of other nations to judge Israel—and to ultimately bring them back to worship Him.

Before Nehemiah ever arrived in Jerusalem, before the work on the walls was even begun, Nehemiah and the people of Israel came under attack from two very wicked and powerful men: Sanballat the Horonite and Tobiah the Ammonite. These men did *not* want Nehemiah and the Israelites to succeed in rebuilding the wall, so they began a campaign against Nehemiah and the people of Jerusalem. It was a campaign built upon one primary tactic: fear.

These fear tactics began as mocking, scornful, verbal attacks against Nehemiah and the people of Jerusalem. Nehemiah responded to their attacks with these courageous words, "The God of heaven will give us success; therefore we His servants will arise and build, but you have no portion, right, or memorial in Jerusalem" (Nehemiah 2:20). Nehemiah was not intimidated by the discouraging words of the enemy. His faith in God superseded any fear he had of mere men.

Sanballat and Tobiah were, however, doggedly persistent. Their fury and anger was further fueled and their fear tactics intensified because of Nehemiah's unwavering dedication to the task of rebuilding. Fear did not paralyze Nehemiah, nor did it prevent him from completing the work to which God had called him. In one of Nehemiah's prayers (Nehemiah 6:9), he wrote the following words about his enemies: "For all of them were trying to frighten us, thinking, 'They will become discouraged with the work and it will not be done.' But now, O God, strengthen my hands." Nehemiah knew the primary motive of the fear tactics of his enemies—to discourage him so that God's mission would not be accomplished.

So much time has passed, so many years have gone by since the days of Nehemiah—but so little has really changed. The same enemy that empowered Sanballat and Tobiah—Satan—is still at work in our world today. His tactics have not changed. Fear continues to be one of his chief weapons of choice as he seeks to intimidate and manipulate us with his threats and accusations. His motive has not changed. It is exactly as it was in Nehemiah's day, "(That we) will become discouraged with the work and it will not be done." God has called us to a great work—to glorify Him and to be His witnesses in a lost and darkened world.

There has never been a time in history when the courageous attributes of Nehemiah are more desperately needed than today. The fear and terror of Islamic extremists has brought the debate about equality and acceptance of all faiths and religions to the forefront. It is not popular in our politically correct culture to quote the uncompromising words of Christ who said, "I am the way, and the truth, and the life; no one comes to the Father, but through me" (John 14:6). But I believe it is time for the church to rebuild the walls of our own faith and to stand up without fear and compromise for the one true God. If we fail to be courageous and stand firm, can we expect God will judge us any less severely than He did when He allowed the armies of Babylon to destroy Jerusalem and take His people captive?

The enemy wants us to keep our mouths shut and to abandon the great work of proclaiming the gospel. He uses fear to keep us mute to the freedoms and opportunities we now have in this country—which we may not have much longer if we fail to act upon them. Fear continues to be a powerfully motivating tool Satan uses against the church of Jesus Christ.

There is, however, a very different and very positive aspect of fear taught in scripture. We see that aspect of fear in Nehemiah's life. In Nehemiah 5:15, he says, "because of the **fear** of God" he was obedient to accomplish God's mission for his life. Nehemiah did not fear the threats of the enemy. Nehemiah did not fear the anger and opinions of men. Nehemiah only feared God. And so should we.

But what does it really mean to fear God? This will be the topic of our study this week. I believe you'll discover fearing the Lord is the key that ultimately opens the door to lasting contentment. In a culture of so-called tolerance, may our prayer today be the same as Nehemiah's:

But now, O God, strengthen (our) hands. Nehemiah 6:9

Day One

1. Spend time in prayer before you begin your study. Ask God to apply the truths you will be studying this week deep within your heart. Commit to Him your willingness to walk according to His ways.

Thou hast ordained Thy precepts, that we should keep them diligently. Psalm 119:4

2. The past three lessons have focused on Solomon's exhortations from Ecclesiastes 3:12–13. These verses are printed below. Please read them, and circle each of the three exhortations you studied in Weeks Six, Seven, and Eight.

> *I know that there is nothing better for them than to rejoice and*
> *to do good in one's lifetime; moreover, that every man who eats*
> *and drinks sees good in all his labor—it is the gift of God.*

3. The final exhortation we will study from Ecclesiastes is found in the very next verse. Ecclesiastes 3:14, which also is printed below. Please read through it, then circle Solomon's exhortation.

> *I know that everything God does will remain forever; there is*
> *nothing to add to it and there is nothing to take from it, for*
> *God has so worked that men should fear Him.*

4. Think about the last phrase in Ecclesiastes 3:14: "for God has so worked that men should fear Him." Ponder this verse prayerfully, then answer the following questions:

   a. How has God "worked that men should fear Him"? In answering this question, it may help to review Solomon's earlier words in Ecclesiastes 1:4–11.

   b. What other works of God would Solomon have personally witnessed in his life? Read 2 Chronicles 1:7–12 and 7:1–3, then record the works Solomon had witnessed earlier in his reign as king.

   c. Briefly explain what you believe Solomon is teaching in Ecclesiastes 3:14.

5. Take a few moments to reflect upon some of the ways you have personally witnessed God's works in the past and in the present. How has God worked and revealed Himself to you in times past? How is God working in your life and revealing Himself to you currently? Record your answers to these questions on the following chart, then complete the sentence that has been started for you at the bottom of the chart:

GOD'S PAST WORKS	GOD'S CURRENT WORKS

I respond to all of God's works by _____

_____

6. Solomon wrote about fearing God in several other verses in Ecclesiastes. Please read the following verses, and record what you learn from them about fearing God:

a.   Ecclesiastes 8:12–13

b.   Ecclesiastes 12:13–14

At this point, I could very easily give you the definition of what it means to fear God. But I don't want to rob you of the experience of discovering it for yourself as He teaches it to you through his Word. You may already have some understanding of what fearing the Lord means. Even so, I pray that as you continue to study, God will deepen your understanding and speak to you personally about the fear of the Lord in a new way.

7.   Undoubtedly, one of the most difficult and emotional experiences ever recorded on the pages of scripture is found in Genesis 22:1–18. Before you read this passage, please try to "slip on Abraham's sandals," and vicariously take the journey he made as the parent of an only child. Please do not read this passage in haste; in fact, read and re-read it. As you read, please journal your own thoughts, feelings, and answers to these questions:

a.   What might Abraham have experienced the night preceding his journey?

b.   What do you think this three-day journey would have been like for Abraham?

c.   What do you believe Abraham's words reveal in verses 5–8?

d.   What do you believe Abraham's actions reveal in verses 9–10?

e.   Why did God require Abraham to go through all of this?

f.   What do you learn about the fear of God from this passage?

g.   How would you define the fear of God according to this passage?

8. Close your time of study by recording your own personal insights. Is God testing you in any area of your life? Is the fear of anything, other than God, preventing you from fully obeying God in any area of your life? Is there any area in your life in which fear often threatens and intimidates you?

_____

_____

_____

_____

_____

_____

_____

_____

_____

Day Two

1. Prepare your heart to study through prayer. Whether you are doing this study with a group or by yourself, use today's Psalm to thank the Lord for the encouragement of your sisters in Christ. Spend some time in intercession for them as well. If you are not currently active in a local church, please pray about this. Ask God to lead you to a Bible-believing church where you can experience fellowship and encouragement with the family of God.

   I am a companion of all those who fear Thee,
   and of those who keep Thy precepts. Psalm 119:63

2. You will continue to study what it means to fear the Lord today. Begin by reading about some incredible, God-fearing women. Please read Exodus 1:8–21, then answer the following questions:

   a. Who spoke to the Hebrew midwives, and what did he tell them?

   b. How did the midwives respond, and what does their response reveal about the fear of the Lord?

   c. What principles does this passage teach about submission to authority?

    d.   What emotions do you think these women might have felt as they twice faced the king? In light of these possible emotions, what does this further reveal about the fear of the Lord?

    e.   According to verses 20–21, what did God do because these women feared Him?

3.   During this same time period in Egypt, two Jewish parents celebrated, in secret, the birth of their son—Moses. Please read this beautiful account in Exodus 2:1–10, then answer the following questions:

    a.   What did you learn about the character of Moses' family from this passage?

    b.   How did you determine their character even though there were no specific attributes, etc., mentioned about them in this passage? In other words, how was their character revealed?

    c.   Record the specific ways God blessed and rewarded the actions of Moses' parents and his sister during the first three months of Moses' life and beyond.

    d.   Hebrews 11:23 gives further insight about Moses' parents. Please read this verse, then briefly summarize what you learn about Moses' parents. How would you describe them?

4.   Many years later, Moses led the sons of Israel out of Egyptian bondage. Please read Exodus 14, and underline each reference to the following words:

fear, feared, frightened, terrified, or *afraid*

NOTE: Depending upon your Bible translation, some of these words may or may not be used.

5. Please summarize below what you learned about fear from Exodus 14:
   a. What are the various types of fear?

   b. What is often the cause of fear?

   c. What are the effects of fear?

   d. What is the "cure" for fear?

6. How does Exodus 14:31 parallel what you learned yesterday from Ecclesiastes 3:14?

7. Quickly review what you studied about Abraham in your homework yesterday, as well as everything you have studied today from Exodus. Think about what you have learned about the fear of the Lord from each of these biblical characters and passages. Compile below a list of five principles or insights you have learned about what it means to fear the Lord.

   The Fear of the Lord Means:

   a. _____

   b. _____

   c. _____

   d. _____

   e. _____

8. As you conclude your study time today, is there an area you believe God would have you apply one or more of the principles you just listed? If so, describe that specific area and the way God is exhorting you to fear Him.

Thy word is a lamp to my feet, and a light to my path.
Psalm 119:105

The unfolding of Thy words gives light.
Psalm 119:130

_____

_____

_____

_____

_____

_____

_____

Day Three

1. Does seeing you or being with you bring joy to the hearts of others? When you are actively trusting and hoping in the Word of God, your life will cause other believers to rejoice—especially as they see you hoping and trusting in God in the midst of a difficult season. Lift up today's Psalm in prayer to God, and proclaim you are placing your hope not in yourself or your own strength, not in another person, and not in your current circumstances—no matter how good or bad they may be. Tell the Lord you are placing your hope solely and completely in Him. Ask Him to allow you to reflect the hope you have in Him to others.

> *May those who fear You rejoice when they see me, for*
> *I have put my hope in Your word.* Psalm 119:74 (NIV)

2. For the past two days you have studied several people who have modeled for you what it means to fear the Lord. As you continue to understand all that it means to fear God, please read the following scriptures (you do not have to take notes from each of them). Observe what they repeatedly teach concerning the result of the fear of God, then complete the sentence written below these verses:

   a. Exodus 20:20
   b. Deuteronomy 5:29
   c. Deuteronomy 6:1–2
   d. Deuteronomy 31:12–13
   e. Acts 10:35
   f. 1 Peter 1:17

   If I truly fear the Lord, I will also _____

   _____ .

3. Please read the following scriptures (you do not have to take notes from each of them). Observe what they repeatedly teach concerning fear, then complete the sentence written below these verses:

    a. Numbers 14:9

    b. Deuteronomy 3:22

    c. 1 Samuel 15:24

    d. Matthew 10:28

    e. 1 Peter 3:14–15

    If I truly fear the Lord, I will also _____

    _____.

4. To further broaden your insight about what it means to fear the Lord, you will now study several scriptures that very succinctly define the fear of the Lord. Please read the scriptures on the following chart, then (using words from the text) record how that scripture defines the fear of the Lord. In the second column, describe what the Lord reveals to you from each of these verses such as: what did you learn about the fear of the Lord, and how would He have you practically apply that verse to your own life?

THE FEAR OF THE LORD IS...	APPLICATION FOR MY LIFE
Psalm 111:10	
Proverbs 1:7	

THE FEAR OF THE LORD IS...	APPLICATION FOR MY LIFE
Proverbs 8:13	
Proverbs 14:27	

5. In your Day Two assignment, page 178, number 7, you made a list of five principles or insights you learned about the fear of the Lord. Please quickly review that list. Also, review what you have learned today about the fear of the Lord. Add five additional principles or insights you have learned about what it means to fear the Lord.

   The Fear of the Lord Means:

   f. _____

   g. _____

   h. _____

   i. _____

   j. _____

Thy word is a lamp to my feet, and a light to my path.
Psalm 119:105

The unfolding of Thy words gives light.
Psalm 119:130

6. Please conclude your day of study by recording any insights you received from the Holy Spirit today that would specifically apply to your life and to your current season of life.

_____

_____

_____

_____

_____

_____

_____

_____

Day Four

1. God has created us for fellowship with Him and for fellowship with other believers. Because of our mutual love and fear of the Lord, believers enjoy a common bond that allows us to experience relationships with one another in a deeply spiritual and satisfying way. As women, we especially long for these kinds of relationships. As you begin your time of study in prayer, ask the Lord to continue to develop your relationship with other sisters in Christ in authentic and accountable ways that will result in further spiritual growth.

May those who fear You turn to me, those who understand Your statutes. Psalm 119:79 (NIV)

2. You have seen the positive side of fear in your lesson this week. The fear of the Lord is a very positive and spiritually rewarding kind of fear. However, the fear Satan uses has a very negative and opposite effect upon our life. Reflect back over the seasons of your life, then list any seasons of fear you may have experienced and how that fear affected you. Also, please describe any ways you experienced deliverance from the bondage of fear.

3. In your current season of life, is the enemy using fear as a tool to defeat you in any way? If so, please describe your current experience with fear.

4. Today, many people are plagued by fear resulting in numerous negative effects upon their lives and the lives of others. Please list some of the ways you have witnessed the negative aspect of fear manifested in today's culture.

I can think of many occasions when fear has threatened to send me into panic mode. Years ago, I used to go shopping with my double-jointed toddler (Kevin, to be specific). He was a "mini Houdini" who could wriggle out of the shoulder and seat restraints in his stroller in no time and then quietly escape. An empty stroller meant instantaneous panic to me as a young mother. As my boys have grown older, anytime the phone rings in the middle of the night, immediately my mind begins conjuring up all kinds of frightening scenarios. Sister, as long as we live, in every season of our lives, there will be aspects of fear we will all experience. We cannot eradicate fear entirely, but we can, by faith, let "the truth set us free" (John 8:32) to experience the supernatural peace of God. Thank God for the truth! Without it, my life as a mom would be one long series of panic attacks.

5. Several passages of scripture give us wonderful truths to claim when fear threatens to overwhelm us. Please read each of the following passages, and record them word-for-word in the space provided:

   a. Psalm 27:1

   b. Psalm 27:5

     c.   Psalm 27:13–14

     d.   Psalm 34:4

     e.   Isaiah 41:10

     f.   Isaiah 43:1–2

     g.   Philippians 4:6–7

6. As you read and recorded each of the previous scriptures, how did they affect you? What impact did their words have upon you? Describe their effect and impact.

7. Choose one of the scriptures listed in number 5 to commit to memory. On a note card or sticky note, please write the scripture you have chosen. Place it on your refrigerator, on your car dashboard, or any place where you will regularly see it. Memorize that scripture, and begin wielding it as your "sword" (Ephesians 6:17) when fear and panic threaten to overwhelm you. Choose to trust and fear God by faith in His Word.

8. The fear of the Lord produces a multitude of benefits and blessings—and none of the bondage that the other types of fear so often produce. Compile a list of the blessings that result from fearing the Lord. Read each scripture, then list each blessing God gives to those who fear Him.

HOW GOD BLESSES THOSE WHO FEAR HIM:

Psalm 33:18   Psalm 115:11

Psalm 34:7   Psalm 145:19

Psalm 103:13   Psalm 147:11

9. Conclude your day of study by recording any specific insights the Holy Spirit has revealed to you.

Thy word is a lamp to my feet, and a light to my path.
Psalm 119:105

The unfolding of Thy words gives light.
Psalm 119:130

Day Five

1. Spend some time with the Lord in prayer before you begin your study. May today's Psalm reflect the deepest desire of your heart.

   Establish Thy word to Thy servant, as that
   which produces reverence for Thee. Psalm 119:38

2. Question: are we to fear the Lord, or are we to *love* the Lord? Is fearing the Lord in any way similar to loving the Lord? Is it possible for these two seemingly opposite concepts to coexist? Please read the following scriptures, and record your insights to the previous questions:

   a. Deuteronomy 10:12–13

   b. Luke 11:42

   c. John 14:23–24

   d. 2 Corinthians 7:1

3. You began your study this week by reviewing Ecclesiastes 3:12–13. The rest of your study this week has concerned Solomon's fourth exhortation found in Ecclesiastes 3:14. In the following blanks, please record the missing word from each of these exhortations:

   1) _____ .—Ecclesiastes 3:12a

   2) _____ good.—Ecclesiastes 3:12b

   3) _____ good.—Ecclesiastes 3:13

   4) _____ God.—Ecclesiastes 3:14

4. Considering everything you have studied about the fear of the Lord, how would Solomon's fourth exhortation affect his first three exhortations? In other words, how would the fourth exhortation be the "key" to "unlocking" the first three exhortations? Explain your answer.

5. Reflect upon all you have learned this week about the fear of the Lord, then write out a very simple and thorough definition of the fear of the Lord by completing the following sentence.

    To fear the Lord means: _____

    _____.

6. Complete your week of study by journaling. Think about all the Lord has taught you this week and how He has spoken to your heart. Include that in your first paragraph. In the second paragraph of your journal, record how you will respond to God.

My Journal

THIS WEEK THE LORD...

_____

_____

_____

_____

_____

_____

_____

_____

_____

AS A RESULT, I...

_____

_____

_____

_____

_____

_____

_____

_____

_____

There is something I must confess to you. Just as I was beginning to write this week's lesson on fearing God, I had a near meltdown in my home office because of…*fear!* Let me give you a little background about what led to my crisis.

Months ago, I was given a deadline to have this study completely written. Months ago, that deadline seemed so distant, so "doable." But there was this one big, giant blind spot I could not see, much less foresee. Having never written anything like this, I was blindly unaware of how much time it would take to develop and to write this course. This was a huge, cavernous blind spot. The deadline came and went and I still hadn't completed the study. By God's glorious grace, the deadline was extended giving me a few more days to write. As I began writing this lesson, the second deadline was looming nearer and nearer—and I *still* hadn't completed this lesson, and I **still** had Week Ten to write.

People often tell me, "Laurie, you always seem so calm and peaceful. Let me tell you, the key word in that statement is "seem." Although I may seem calm, and I may seem tranquil, the truth is, I may be one small step from a major "meltdown." No one can visibly see the knots in my neck and shoulders. No one can actually see the anxiety within my heart. But I'm aware of it, and God is very much aware of it.

These meltdowns of mine are usually very small, private affairs, and the other day I was alone in my house. With each passing hour, my second deadline was inching nearer and nearer. I could feel the stress in my body. I could hear the fearful taunts and threats of the enemy. I could endure it no longer—I broke.

On my knees in my office, I poured out my complaint, my fears, and my weakness before the Lord. I confessed to Him my sin for allowing fear and anxiety to consume and control me (the very week I was writing a lesson on fear). Then I claimed His promises to me—"Faithful is He that calleth you, who also will do it" (1 Thessalonians 5:24 KJV), and "I can do all things through (Christ) who strengthens me" (Philippians 4:13). I was a blubbery, weepy mess. But when I arose from my knees, I immediately recognized God had lifted my burden and renewed my strength.

I conclude with one final confession to you, my sister: God's Word works! If we are full of anxiety, if we are paralyzed by fear, it is not because God cannot free us—it is because we fear something or someone instead of fearing God. The fear of the Lord is the key that unlocks the door to a life of freedom and contentment in **every** season.

Glory to God! Praise His wonderful name! Rejoice and stand in awe of the One who delivers us from all of our fears! Onward I go in victory to write Week Ten!

The Key to Contentment

I.   **Principles of** _____ :

    A.   Submit to the _____. *Ecc. 3:1–11*

        1. _____

        2. _____

        3. _____

        4. _____

    B.   Practice the _____. *Ecc. 3:12–13*

        1. _____

        2. _____

        3. _____

    C.   Use the _____.

II.   **Scripture teaches we are to fear the Lord because:**

    A.   His works and His ways are _____ and _____. *Ecc. 3:14*

    B.   _____ will be _____ for those who fear Him, and _____ will **not** be _____ for those who do not fear Him. *Ecc. 8:12–13*

    C.   It is the final conclusion, the _____ _____ that applies to every person. *Ecc. 12:13*

    D.   It is linked to _____ God / _____ His commandments. *Ecc. 12:13*

    E.   God will bring every _____ to _____. *Ecc. 12:14*

III. **What does it mean to fear the Lord?:**

    A. It involves **BOTH** _____ and _____.

        1. _____: _____ to God because of His power and position.

        2. _____: results in the _____ to please Him **AND** the _____ to obey Him.

    B. Therefore, if I say I fear the Lord I will _____ **AND** _____ Him.

IV. **Three who feared the Lord:**

    A. _____ _Gen. 6:5–9, 13, 22, Heb. 11:7_

    B. _____ _Gen. 22:1–3, 5, 12, 15–18_

    C. _____ _____ _Ex. 1:17, 21_

These examples reveal that _____, _____, _____, _____, and blessing are all characteristics of those who fear the Lord.

V. **Choosing Contentment:**

    A. I _cannot_ unlock the doors to contentment by…

      • waiting until I _____ _____ rejoicing,

      • waiting for my _____ or my _____ to improve before I do good,

      • or waiting until I can _____ the value of all I'm doing.

    B. I _can_ unlock the doors to contentment when I _____ to…

      • rejoice,

      • do good,

      • and see good
because I _____ _____.

The Harmony of Proverbs 31 and Ecclesiastes 1

A beautiful blessing and promise has been given to us in Psalm 1:1–3:

How blessed is the man who does not walk in the counsel of the wicked, nor stand in the path of sinners, nor sit in the seat of scoffers! But his delight is in the law of the Lord, and in His law he meditates day and night. And he will be like a tree firmly planted by streams of water, which yields its fruit in its season, and its leaf does not wither; and in whatever he does, he prospers.

Allow me to give you my personal paraphrase of that passage: When we willfully deny ungodliness to influence and guide our lives and willingly allow God's Word to be our primary influence, our spiritual "roots" will deepen allowing us to grow, produce spiritual fruit, and prosper in every season of life. Wow! What a promise!

With Psalm 1:1–3 in mind, let me ask you a question. Have you ever been around someone who has been a Christian for many years, yet they're miserable, complaining, bitter, and unhappy? I'm talking about people who have been in church for ages. They know the Bible backward and forward. They may even be "pillars" in the church. How does this happen? Or is this even possible? You may think it is not possible. You may believe these kinds of people were never genuinely saved. That may well be, but I think there could be another reason.

Christians who choose to be influenced and led by their own fleshly desires are usually the most miserable people on the planet. Furthermore, Christians who do not give God's Word priority in their lives *will not mature* which means they often behave like selfish, spoiled children. However, even Christians who diligently study God's Word but fail to consistently apply it can become proud, self-consumed, and very dissatisfied.

This week you will return to the pages of Proverbs 31 and Ecclesiastes 1 for one final look at the Model Woman and King Solomon. These two very opposite people, in two very different books of the Bible, surprisingly have a great deal in common. They stand beside one another in the "songbook" of scripture—the Model Woman on one page and Solomon on the next page. They share the same music, but only one of them is truly "singing" it.

My sister, in every season of your life, may you produce the spiritual fruit of godliness and contentment because you choose to "sing" His Word.

Day One

1. Prepare your heart in prayer before you begin your study. As you approach God, ask Him to reveal whether or not your heart is fully devoted to Him. Thank Him for His unending grace, and commit to follow Him wholeheartedly.

    I entreated Thy favor with all my heart; be gracious to me according to Thy Word. Psalm 119:58

2. You began this study many weeks ago by reading Proverbs 31:10–31 and Ecclesiastes 1. Please read both of these passages, then:

    a. Underline Proverbs 31:18a, 25b, and Ecclesiastes 1:8.

    b. Please describe any contrast you see between the verses you underlined in Proverbs and the verse you underlined in Ecclesiastes.

    c. Listed below are two incomplete statements. Please complete them by filling in each blank with a word you feel would be appropriate.

    According to the Proverbs 31 Woman, life is _____.

    According to Solomon in Ecclesiastes 1, life is _____.

3. The definitions for "satisfy" and "content" are listed below for you to review. Also, the definitions for the Hebrew words "full" and "fill" are provided. As you read through each definition, note the similarity between each of these words. Understanding the similarity between these words will help you as you complete your homework this week.

    a. **satisfy/satisfied**: to sate, i.e. fill to satisfaction (lit. or fig.): have enough, satisfy.[21]

    b. **content**: satisfied; happy.[22]

    c. **fill/full**: to fill; or the filling of something that was empty; the experience of satiation.[23]

    d. **fill/full**: to fill, or be full; fullness, overflow, satisfy.[24]

4. Listed below are two columns of scriptures that contain the words "satisfy/satisfied," "content/contentment," and "filled." Please circle each one of these words as you read through each column of scriptures. In the space provided under each column, please write a brief statement summarizing the primary teaching of the scriptures in each column.

SCRIPTURAL TRUTHS ABOUT SATISFACTION AND CONTENTMENT

All things are wearisome; man is not able to tell it. The eye is not satisfied with seeing, nor is the ear filled with hearing. **Ecclesiastes 1:8**	As for me, I shall behold Thy face in righteousness, I will be satisfied with Thy likeness when I awake. **Psalm 17:15**
There was a certain man without a dependent, having neither a son nor a brother, yet there was no end to all his labor. Indeed, his eyes were not satisfied with riches and he never asked, 'And for whom am I laboring and depriving myself of pleasure?' This too is vanity and it is a grievous task. **Ecclesiastes 4:8**	But godliness actually is a means of great gain, when accompanied by contentment. For we have brought nothing into the world, so we cannot take anything out of it either. And if we have food and covering, with these we shall be content. **1 Timothy 6:6–8**
He who loves money will not be satisfied with money, nor he who loves abundance with its income. This too is vanity. **Ecclesiastes 5:10**	Let your character be free from the love of money, being content with what you have, for He Himself has said, 'I WILL NEVER DESERT YOU, NOR WILL I EVER FORSAKE YOU.' **Hebrews 13:5**
If a man fathers a hundred children and lives many years, however many they be, but his soul is not satisfied with good things, and he does not even have a proper burial, then I say, 'Better the miscarriage than he.' **Ecclesiastes 6:3**	The fear of the Lord leads to life, so that one may sleep satisfied, untouched by evil. **Proverbs 19:23**
All a man's labor is for his mouth and yet the appetite is not satisfied. **Ecclesiastes 6:7**	For He has satisfied the thirsty soul, and the hungry soul He has filled with what is good. **Psalm 107:9**

Summary Statement:

_____

_____

_____

Summary Statement:

_____

_____

_____

5. The scriptures you just read from Ecclesiastes are, of course, Solomon's words. As you quickly scan them, does Solomon reveal any source of lasting satisfaction? What does this reveal to you about Solomon's spiritual life, especially in light of the second column of scriptures?

6. Exodus 16:1–18 is a passage that contains the words "filled" and "full," which were defined for you. Please underline these words in your Bible as you read this passage, then answer the following questions. **NOTE: The NIV Bible translates these words as "all the food we wanted," and as "all the bread you want."**

   a. According to verses 2, 8, and 12, how were the Israelites expressing themselves and why were they expressing themselves in this way?

   b. According to verse 3, what had satisfied them in Egypt?

   c. According to verses 6–8, what did Moses promise the people? What experience did he tell them they would have?

   d. According to verse 4, why did God ration their food to them daily?

   e. In light of the words you underlined in your Bible and their definitions, what else do you believe God was trying to teach His people through this process and experience?

7. In all honesty, please answer the following questions:

    a.   Can you relate to the Israelites in the Exodus 16 passage in any way in your current season of life? Have you been grumbling or murmuring about anything recently or on an ongoing basis? Is there an area in your life in which you are not satisfied?

    b.   What do you believe God is trying to teach you through the circumstances of your current season? What might be His reason for not allowing your circumstances to change or improve?

Insights

8. Please list any insights the Holy Spirit has given you through your study today as well as how you desire to respond to His promptings.

Thy word is a lamp to my feet, and a light to my path.
Psalm 119:105

The unfolding of Thy words gives light.
Psalm 119:130

_____

_____

_____

_____

_____

_____

_____

Day Two

1. Begin your study time in prayer using the words of today's Psalm to express your heart to the Lord.

> *May my heart be blameless in Thy statutes,*
> *that I may not be ashamed.* Psalm 119:80

As you saw in your study yesterday, Solomon and the Model Woman had very different perspectives on life. But did they differ in their beliefs about God? Did they differ in what they believed about practicing their faith?

2. Today you will study Solomon and learn more about his knowledge of God and his relationship with God. Please read the following scriptures and passages about Solomon, and record what you learn about: his spiritual training and life, his encounters with God, his beliefs in God, and his wealth:

DEUTERONOMY 17:14–20
A RECORD OF GOD'S INSTRUCTIONS FOR ISRAEL'S KINGS:

a. Summarize God's various commandments to all of Israel's kings from verses 16–17.

b. According to this passage, what spiritual training would Solomon have had. Also, how long was a king required to read God's law and, most importantly, why?

1 KINGS 3:1–14, 6:11–14, 8:22–43, 54–61
SOLOMON'S RELATIONSHIP AND EARLY ENCOUNTERS WITH GOD

a. What did you learn about Solomon's relationship with God from 1 Kings 3?

b. According to 1 Kings 3:14, what did God require and promise Solomon?

c. According to 1 Kings 6:11–14, what did God further require and promise Solomon?

d. According to 1 Kings 8:22–26, what did Solomon believe about God, and what did he know about the importance of practicing his faith?

e. According to 1 Kings 8:38–40, what did Solomon believe about God and what did he believe men should do?

f. According to 1 Kings 8:54–61, what did Solomon pray for his people and for himself?

1 Kings 9:1–9
Solomon's Second Encounter with God

a. According to verses 1–3, how did God respond to Solomon's earlier prayer at the dedication of the temple in 1 Kings 8? What did God promise Solomon?

b. According to verses 4–5, what did God promise Solomon?

c. According to verses 6–9, what was God's warning to Solomon?

1 KINGS 4:25–26, 10:14–29
SOLOMON'S WEALTH

a.   According to 1 Kings 4 and 10, summarize some of Solomon's possessions.

b.   According to what you previously learned from Deuteronomy 17:16a, what had Solomon ignored, and what does that reveal about his faith and practice?

c.   What did you learn about Solomon in 1 Kings 10:23?

Thy word is a lamp to my feet, and a light to my path.
Psalm 119:105

The unfolding of Thy words gives light.
Psalm 119:130

Insights

3.   How has the Holy Spirit spoken to your heart today? What insights has He given you as you have studied the beginning of Solomon's life?

_____

_____

_____

_____

_____

_____

_____

_____

There is a Season

Day Three

1. Today's Psalm is so beautiful and so appropriate—especially in light of what you studied yesterday and what you will study today. Make the words of this Psalm your prayer before God.

> *I have inclined my heart to perform Thy*
> *statutes forever, even to the end.* Psalm 119:112

2. Complete your study on Solomon's life by reading the following passage and recording what you learn about his latter years as king:

1 KINGS 11:1–14
SOLOMON'S LATTER YEARS AS KING

a. According to these verses, what specific things did Solomon do that were forbidden by God, and what was the result in his own faith and practice?

b. According to verses 9–13, what were God's last recorded words to Solomon?

c. According to verse 14, what did God do?

3. Please read the following scriptures. Note the two key words used in two of them regarding Abraham and David's deaths but that are not used in describing Solomon's death. Please circle these words.

> *And Abraham breathed his last and died in a ripe old age, an old man and satisfied with life.* Genesis 25:8

> *Then (David) died in a ripe old age, full of days, riches and honor; and his son Solomon reigned in his place.* 1 Chronicles 29:28

> *And Solomon slept with his fathers and was buried in the city of his father, David.* 1 Kings 11:43

4. What do the key words mentioned in Genesis 25:8 and 1 Chronicles 29:28 reveal about Abraham and David? Why do you think these words were omitted from Solomon's obituary in 1 Kings?

5. Based on yesterday and today's study of Solomon, answer the following questions:

   a. Did Solomon truly have a relationship with God? If so, briefly describe what you believe occurred in Solomon's relationship with God as he grew older.

   b. Earlier in Solomon's life, do you believe he truly feared the Lord? Please explain your answer.

c.   Do you believe Solomon truly feared the Lord in the latter years of his life? Please explain your answer.

6. In Solomon's latter years, when he most likely wrote Ecclesiastes, he instructed others with the following wise principles and exhortations concerning how to live and practice their faith. Please read and review these principles and exhortations:

FOUR TRUTHS ABOUT LIFE

1. Ecclesiastes 3:1–8—There is a season for everything in life.

2. Ecclesiastes 3:11a—God has made everything beautiful, appropriate, and with purpose in its time.

3. Ecclesiastes 3:11b—God has made us long for eternal significance and meaning in our lives.

4   Ecclesiastes 3:11c—We cannot yet fully know the eternal significance, value, and purpose of our lives.

FOUR EXHORTATIONS

1. Ecclesiastes 3:12a—Rejoice

2. Ecclesiastes 3:12b—Do good

3. Ecclesiastes 3:13—See good

4   Ecclesiastes 3:14—Fear God

7. Considering everything you have studied about Solomon, do you believe he was practicing the truths and exhortations above at the time he wrote them?

Please circle one: **yes   no**

8. Do you believe Solomon's teachings are true even though he may not have practiced them himself?

Please circle one: **yes   no**

9. Considering everything you have studied about the Model Woman from Proverbs 31, do you believe she practiced these truths and exhortations in her life?

Please circle one: **yes   no**

10. Solomon's four exhortations are listed in the following chart. Please read through Proverbs 31:10–31, and record (using words from the text) how the Model Woman practiced these exhortations:

HOW THE MODEL WOMAN PRACTICES HER FAITH

Rejoice
Do Good
See Good
Fear God

Insights

11. Has the Lord spoken to you as you have studied the faith and practice of Solomon and the Model Woman? Please record the insights He's revealed to your heart today.

Thy word is a lamp to my feet, and a light to my path.
Psalm 119:105

The unfolding of Thy words gives light.
Psalm 119:130

_____

_____

_____

_____

_____

_____

_____

Day Four

1. Begin your study time today in prayer expressing to God, as the psalmist did, your love for His Word and your commitment to practicing it throughout your lifetime.

Pray

> *My soul keeps Thy testimonies, and*
> *I love them exceedingly.* Psalm 119:167

2. The harmony of Proverbs 31:10–31 and Ecclesiastes 1 is found in the practice of the Model Woman and in the exhortations of Solomon. As you have studied the Model Woman and Solomon, you have seen they believed the very same things. But only the Model Woman truly practiced her beliefs throughout her lifetime. If Solomon had practiced the truth he believed, the legacy of his life would have been so different.

God's final words to Solomon are recorded in 1 Kings 11:11–13. God's final words describing the Model Woman are in Proverbs 31:29–31. Both of these passages are printed below. Please read through them.

> *So the Lord said to Solomon, "Because you have done this, and you have not kept My covenant and My statutes, which I have commanded you, I will surely tear the kingdom from you, and will give it to your servant. Nevertheless, I will not do it in your days, for the sake of your father David, but I will tear it out of the hand of your son. However, I will not tear away all the kingdom, but I will give one tribe to your son for the sake of My servant David and for the sake of Jerusalem which I have chosen."* 1 Kings 11:11–13

> *Many daughters have done nobly, but you excel them all. Charm is deceitful and beauty is vain, but a woman who fears the Lord, she shall be praised. Give her the product of her hands, and let her works praise her in the gates.* Proverbs 31:29–31

There is a Season

3. Based on 1 Kings 11:11–13, briefly describe the legacy of Solomon. How did his life affect the next generation? How will he always be remembered?

4. Based on Proverbs 31:29–31, briefly describe the legacy of the Model Woman. How do you think her life will affect the next generation? How do you think she will always be remembered?

We all want to leave a legacy like that of the Model Woman, and because of Christ, we can. Over the past several years, I have begun to refer to the first three exhortations from Ecclesiastes 3:12–13— "rejoice, do good, see good"—as "The Three Doors to Contentment." In order to help you remember these truths, please write one of the exhortations from Ecclesiastes 3:12–13 on each of the three following "doors." You'll also see a "key." Please write the fourth exhortation on it.

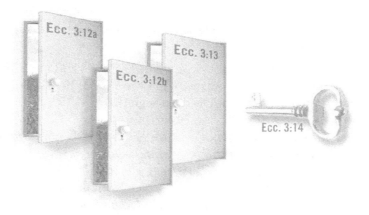

I hope this illustration will enable you to remember the four key truths of this study so that you can experience contentment in every season of your life. I have this illustration etched into my mind. As soon as the Lord convicts me of grumbling or a negative attitude, I am reminded to pick up the key—fear God—and to obey Him reverently by rejoicing, doing good, and seeing good in my life. And if I can experience contentment, sister, you can, too!

5. In order to reinforce the Three Doors to Contentment and The Key to Contentment, you will be reading the brief, four-chapter book of Philippians today. Since you read this book several weeks ago (Week 6), you may be wondering why you need to read it again. Here's why: Paul is a role model of contentment. In fact, he even says, "I have learned to be content in whatever circumstances I am" (Philippians 4:11).

Read Philippians, and make brief notes under the following headings about how Paul is practicing The Three Doors to Contentment and The Key to Contentment as he writes this book during a difficult season he spent in *prison.*

Paul's example of:
The Fear of the Lord

_____

_____

_____

_____

_____

_____

_____

_____

_____

_____

Paul's example of:
Rejoicing

_____

_____

_____

_____

_____

_____

_____

_____

_____

_____

Paul's example of:
Doing Good

_____

_____

_____

_____

_____

_____

_____

_____

_____

Paul's example of:
Seeing Good

_____

_____

_____

_____

_____

_____

_____

_____

_____

*Thy word is a lamp
to my feet, and a
light to my path.*
Psalm 119:105

*The unfolding of Thy
words gives light.*
Psalm 119:130

6. As you conclude your study for today, how has the Lord spoken to you through the example of the Model Woman and/or Paul?

_____

_____

_____

_____

_____

_____

_____

_____

Day Five

1. In this final day of your study, let your prayer be full of praise and thanksgiving for God's faithfulness in teaching you His Word these past ten weeks. Praise Him for the specific things He has taught you. Praise Him for His love and patience toward you. Ask Him to enable you to remember The Three Doors to Contentment and The Key that unlocks each door in every season. Praise Him for the way He has renewed and transformed you through the power of His Word and the empowerment of His Spirit.

*I will praise You with an upright heart as
I learn Your righteous laws.* Psalm 119:7 (NIV)

Your study will be light today in order to give you more time for your final journaling experience in this study. Right now, if possible, pick up your Bible, pen, and this workbook, and move to the most comfortable, quiet room in your house. With your Bible in your lap, drink in the scriptures—personalize and read them aloud to the Lord. Read them as if they were written just for you—because they were. Enjoy your final day of this study with Him.

2. Please read the following scriptures and observe what they teach you about the fullness of God's satisfaction.

   a. Psalm 22:25–26

   b. Psalm 63:1–8

     c.   Psalm 65:4

     d.   Psalm 81:10

     e.   Psalm 103:1–14

     f.   Psalm 145:16–19

     g.   Matthew 5:6

     h.   John 6:30–35, 48–51

3. After reading those wonderful scriptures, take a few moments to rejoice silently in your spirit or aloud to the Lord your God who satisfies.

4. Think about your current season of life, and briefly record your thoughts about the following questions:

     a.   In what specific ways do you believe God would have you "rejoice" (Ecclesiastes 3:12) in this season of life?

     b.   In what specific ways do you believe God would have you "do good" (Ecclesiastes 3:12) in this season of life? What would He desire to be the focus of your life and ministry in this season?

     c.   In what specific ways do you believe God would have you "see good" (Ecclesiastes 3:13) and accept this season as appropriate and as having a good purpose for you? How would He desire you to enjoy this season of your life?

    d.   Will you respond to all the Lord has shown you by using The Key to Contentment, and by obeying His commands in this season of your life?

Please circle your answer: yes   no

5.   Spend the rest of your time today journaling. Reflect back upon everything the Lord has taught you during this brief ten-week season of study. Be sensitive and allow the Holy Spirit to guide your thoughts as you journal.

My Journal

OVER THE LAST TEN WEEKS THE LORD…

_____

_____

_____

_____

_____

_____

_____

_____

_____

_____

_____

_____

AS A RESULT, I…

_____

_____

_____

_____

_____

_____

_____

_____

_____

_____

_____

_____

Asong has been playing in my mind for the past several days. It's an old hymn I learned many years ago. I believe the Holy Spirit has brought it to mind to share with you as we mark the conclusion of our study together.

I am satisfied with Jesus, He has done so much for me:
He has suffered to redeem me, He has died to set me free.

I am satisfied, I am satisfied, I am satisfied with Jesus,
But the question comes to me, as I think of Calvary,
Is my Master satisfied with me?[25]

The life Christ died to give us is joyful, meaningful, and deeply satisfying because *He satisfies.* The pointed, direct question of the lyrics above should cause each of us, however, to ask ourselves, *"Is my Master satisfied with me?"*[26]

You have looked into the perfect mirror of God's Word for many weeks now. You have studied the seasons of life and how you can become a reflection of His radiance in every season. I wonder. What did you see when you looked into God's mirror ten weeks ago? But even more importantly, what do you see now?

God's Word is immutable—it does not change. We, on the other hand, are commanded to change and "be transformed" (Romans 12:2). When we allow Him to change and transform us, we will find true and lasting satisfaction in Him, and He will be satisfied with us.

My heart's desire for you, my sister, is that you would choose contentment in every remaining season of your life by accepting God's glorious invitation and promise to you: *"Open your mouth wide and I will fill it"* (Psalm 81:10).

The Harmony of Proverbs 31 and Ecclesiastes 1

I.   **You should not be content with…**

    A. An _____ _____. *Gen. 2:18–25, Col. 3:18–19, Eph. 5:22–29, 1 Cor. 7:10–15*

    B. Any _____ _____ in your life. *1 John 3:9, 1 John 1:9*

    C. A lack of _____ _____. *1 Pet. 2:2, 2 Pet. 3:18*

    D. Anything less than _____-_____ devotion and love for the Lord. *Matt. 22:37*

II. **Evaluating the Model Woman and Solomon**

    In Every Season of Life…

The Model Woman	Solomon
❑ Possessed genuine faith in God	❑ Possessed genuine faith in God
❑ Believed God's commands	❑ Believed God's commands
❑ Practiced God's commands	❑ Practiced God's commands
❑ Feared God	❑ Feared God
❑ Experienced joy and meaning in life	❑ Experienced joy and meaning in life
❑ Experienced satisfaction/contentment	❑ Experienced satisfaction/contentment

    Their legacies…

The Model Woman's life is an _____ for all of us to _____ because she chose to _____ and _____ the Lord fully throughout every season of her life.

Solomon's life is a _____ for all of us to _____ because he chose not to _____ and _____ the Lord fully throughout every season of his life.

III.   **Following God Fully**

A.   **The Example:** *Christ*

1.   He fully _____ Himself of His _____ as God. *Phil 2:5-7*

2.   He fully _____ all righteousness. *Matt. 3:15*

3.   He fully _____ each of His miracles. *Matt. 4:23, 8:16, 14:20, John 2:3–10*

4.   He fully _____ the penalty of our sin. *John 19:30*

B.   **The Motive:** *Jesus fully gave so that we could experience _____ to the _____. John 10:10*

C.   **The Call:** *"_____ _____" is Jesus' high call to us. Matt. 4:19, 8:22*

D.   **The Requirements:**

1.   _____ love. *Matt. 10:37*

2.   _____. *Matt. 10:38*

3.   Self-_____. *Matt. 10:39*

E.   **The Result:** *Those who fully follow Christ throughout every season of their lives will experience "life to the full"—_____ and _____ in this life—and they will leave _____ _____ for others to follow.*

Notes

WEEK ONE—She Said He Said

[1] Copyright 2001 by Houghton Mifflin Company. Reproduced by permission from *The American Heritage Dictionary, Fourth Paperback Edition.*

[2] Ibid.

[3] James Strong, *Strong's Exhaustive Concordance* (Iowa Falls, Iowa: Riverside Book and Bible House), 1892. Used by permission of Thomas Nelson, Inc.

WEEK THREE—THE SEASONS OF DAVID'S LIFE

[4] Spiros Zodhiates, et al., eds., *The Complete Word Study Old Testament* (Chattanooga, TN: AMG Publishers, 1994), #6256, 2353.

WEEK FIVE—THE SEASONS OF YOUR LIFE

[5] Taken from *My Utmost for His Highest by Oswald Chambers*, © 1935 by Dodd, Mead & Co., renewed © 1963 by Oswald Chambers Publications Assn., Ltd. Used by permission of Discovery House Publishers, Box 3566, Grand Rapids, MI 49501. All rights reserved.

[6] Ibid.

[7] Ibid.

WEEK SIX—REJOICING IN EVERY SEASON

[8] Lewis E Jones (1865-1936), "There is Power in the Blood."

[9] Isaac Watts (1674-1748), "We're Marching to Zion."

[10] Jones, "There is Power in the Blood."

[11] James Strong, *Strong's Exhaustive Concordance* (Iowa Falls, Iowa: Riverside Book and Bible House), 1892. Used by permission of Thomas Nelson, Inc.

[12] Ibid, 7646.

[13] Copyright © 2001 by Houghton Mifflin Company. Reproduced by permission from *The American Heritage Dictionary, Fourth Paperback Edition.*

[14] Warren Baker, gen. ed., *The Complete Word Study Old Testament* (Chattanooga: AMG Publishers, 1994), p. 1641.

[15] Taken from *Baxter's Explore the Book* by J. Sidlow Baxter, Copyright © by J. Sidlow Baxter. Used by permission of The Zondervan Corporation.

[16] James Strong. *Strong's Exhaustive Concordance* (Iowa Falls, Iowa: Riverside Book and Bible House), 8055.

WEEK EIGHT—SEEING GOOD IN EVERY SEASON

[17] James Strong, *Strong's Exhaustive Concordance* (Iowa Falls, Iowa: Riverside Book and Bible House), 7200. Used by permission of Thomas Nelson, Inc.

[18] Warren Baker, gen. ed., *The Complete Word Study Old Testament* (Chattanooga: AMG Publishers, 1994), p. 233.

[19] Strong, *Strong's Exhaustive Concordance*, 2896.

[20] Baker, *The Complete Word Study Old Testament*, p. 2320.

WEEK TEN—THE HARMONY OF PROVERBS 31 AND ECCLESIASTES 1

[21] James Strong, *Strong's Exhaustive Concordance* (Iowa Falls: Riverside book and Bible House), 7646. Used by permission of Thomas Nelson, Inc.

[22] Copyright © 2001 by Houghton Mifflin Company. Reproduced by permission from *The American Heritage Dictionary, Fourth Paperback Edition.*

[23] Warren Baker, gen. ed., *The Complete Word Study Old Testament* (Chattanooga: AMG Publishers, 1994), p. 2332.

[24] Strong, *Strong's Exhaustive Concordance*, 4390.

[25] B.B. McKinney, *The Baptist Hymnal* (Nashville, TN: Convention Press, 1991), p. 472; © 1926, 1953, Broadman Press (SESAC). Used by permission.

[26] Ibid.

ShopPriority

Visit Priority's online store to find out more about Bible studies, DVDs, and CDs by Laurie Cole. Each product will encourage you to give God glory and priority.

Shop online now!
Monday - Friday, 9am - 4pm CST

www.priorityministries.org/shop

AUDIO CD SETS

BEAUTY BY THE BOOK &
BEAUTY BY THE BOOK *FOR TEENS*
Bible Studies

THE TEMPLE
Bible Study

Priority's
"you glo, girl"
Bible study will
help you discover
how to *glo*–glorify God.

New!
FREE
Video Downloads
for both *Beauty by The Book* studies!

Whether
you're 17 or 70,
learn the secrets
of becoming
a biblically
beautiful
woman.

Resources available for these studies:
Workbooks, Small Group CD-ROM Leader Guides,
Video Lectures and Audio Lectures.

YouGLOGirl

Priority Ministries' **monthly e-newsletter**, is our opportunity to *glo*–to give God glory–as Laurie Cole and the Priority staff share the latest scoop about Priority Ministries. Visit us online to *subscribe* or read the latest issue.

www.priorityministries.org/glogirl

ConnectWithPriority

Priority Partners believe in the mission of Priority Ministries and support it with their generous financial gifts. Would you prayerfully consider becoming a Partner and helping us reach and teach women to love God most and seek Him first?

Become a monthly or one-time donor. Either way, your financial gifts provide vital support for this ministry! For more information about becoming a Priority Partner, visit our web site:

www.priorityministries.org/support

PrioritySorority

Sisters encouraging sisters to give God priority.

Priority Sorority is an online bulletin board where you can post your praise to God for the way He is working in your life, or read what others are saying about a Priority Bible Study. So, c'mon...join today! Become a Priority Sorority Sister!

How to join:

Visit our web site, www.priorityministries.org, click the *Connect with Priority* link, and click on *Priority Sorority Bulletin Board* to:

- Share your testimony.
- Read other testimonies.
- Be encouraged!

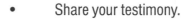

www.priorityministries.org/connect/sorority/sharebboard.php

Priority Ministries

Encouraging Women to Give God Glory & Priority